A Land to Die For

◆ **Binka Le Breton** ◆

Clarity Press, Inc.

ISBN: 0-932863-24-8

Cover photo: Binka Le Breton
Photo of Padre Josimo: J. R. Ripper/Imagens da Terra.
In-house Editor: Diana G. Collier

LCCCN: 97-066910

Cataloguing in Publication Data:

Le Breton, Binka.
    A land to die for / Binka Le Breton. -- 1st ed.
    p. cm.
    Includes bibliographical references and index.
    ISBN: 0-932863-24-8

1. Land reform--Brazil--Goiás (State). 2. Brazil--Social conditions. 3. Josimo, Padre, 1953-1986--Assassination. 4. Catholic Church--Brazil. I. Title.

HD1333.B73L43 1997   333.3'181'73
                                       QB197-40609

CLARITY PRESS, INC.
Ste. 469, 3277 Roswell Rd. N.E.
Atlanta, GA. 30305
Toll free order: 1-800-533-0301
Bulk order: 1-800-626-4330
Internet: http://www.bookmasters.com/clarity
E-mail: clarity@islandnet.com

◆ Table of Contents ◆

✦ List of Characters ✦

Brazilian names are so long and complex that most people only use one or two, either their first name or a nickname. Courtesy titles such as "Dona" or "Padre" are also used, but not invariably.

GROUP ONE: Josimo's closest associates
  Josimo (Josimo Morais Tavares) pronounced Joh-zee'-mo parish priest of São Sebastião
  Dona Olinda his mother, São Sebastião
  Domingos (Domingos Furlan) his assistant, São Sebastião
  Edna (Edna Pereira da Silva) his catechist, São Sebastião
  Mada (Madeleine Huaiss) French nun, Mulatos
  Bia (Beatriz Kruch) French nun, Mulatos
  Lurdinha (Lurdes Lúcia Gói) Brazilian former nun, Buriti

GROUP TWO: Village leaders and activists
  Dona Raimunda (Raimunda Gomes da Silva) union leader, Sete Barracas
  Joâo Custódio union leader, Sumauma
  Maria Senhora (Maria Senhora Carvalho da Silva) union leader, Mulatos
  Natividade (Natividade de Oliveira) union leader, Sampaio
  Dona Cota, village activist, Esperantina
  Mara and *Joâo Ananias*, village activists, Buriti

GROUP THREE: Clergy
  Dom Aloísio (Aloísio Hilário Pinho) bishop of Tocantinópolis
  Padre Mariano (Mariano Sobrinho Souza) parish priest, Tocantinópolis
  Padre Carmelo (Carmelo Scampa) Italian seminary director, Tocantinópolis
  Padre Miguel, Josimo's successor in São Sebastião

GROUP FOUR: Associates in the land struggle
  Amparo (Maria Amparo Cardoso) church worker, Imperatriz
  Perpétua (Maria Perpétua Marinho) church worker, Imperatriz

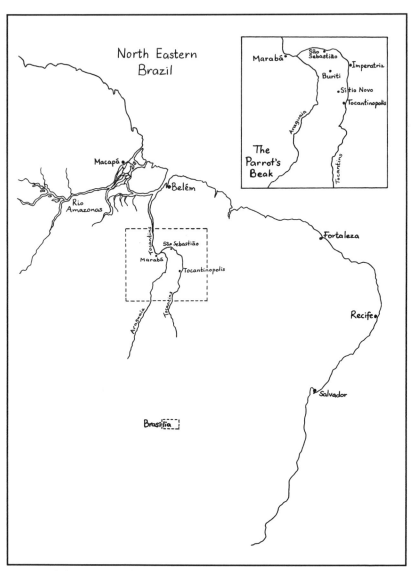

Hand-drawn map of North Eastern Brazil courtesy of Amanda Le Breton

Xavier (Brother Xavier Plassat) French friar, CPT, Sítio Novo
Carlinhos (Carlinhos Furlan) roving agronomist, Imperatriz
Adilar (Adilar Daltoé) CPT lawyer, Gurupi
Pedro Luis (Pedro Luis Dalcero) former CPT lawyer, Imperatriz
Pedro Tierra (a.k.a. Hamilton Pereira) ex-CPT, poet, dissident.

GROUP FIVE : Josimo's enemies
   Geraldo (Geraldo Rodrigues da Costa) *pistoleiro* who killed Josimo (jailed)
   Vilson (Vilson Nunes Cardoso) his accomplice (escaped from jail)
   Nenem (Osmar Teodoro da Silva) instigator of the crime
   Temtem (Guiomar Teodoro da Silva) instigator of the crime
   Mundico (Osvaldo Teodoro da Silva) instigator of the crime
   Joâo (Joâo Teodoro da Silva) instigator of the crime
   Deca (Nazaré Teodoro da Silva) instigator of the crime
   Geraldo Nó (Geraldo Vieira) instigator of the crime
   Adailson (Adailson Vieira) his son, instigator of the crime

Joâo Olímpio, former deputy mayor of São Sebastião, now mayor of Buriti
Zé Carneiro, mayor of São Sebastião

✦ **Introduction** ✦

All over the world, people are fighting for land. Fighting for a place to live in peace, a place to raise their children, a place for the heart to be happy. Rwanda, Palestine, Ireland, Kashmir — the list goes on and on. Small countries, large countries, legacies of fear, legacies of hate.

In the Americas, we hear of renewed land struggles in Mexico, guerrilla fighting in Colombia and Peru, and recurring problems in Central America. But we don't hear much of a small but deadly war that is going on in the Brazilian countryside, a war that claims hundreds of lives every year. A war over what? A war over land.

Brazil is an enormous country, with a relatively small population and plenty of land to go round. Why, then, a land war? Part of the problem stems from the shocking inequalities in the distribution of wealth and possessions. The rich have the lion's share of the money, the land, and the power. Because they are so rich and powerful, many consider themselves to be above the law.

This attitude is historically based. The first lands granted by the Portuguese crown were so vast and so remote that the landowners exercised virtual dominion over those who lived in and around their estates. In the culture of the frontier, the law that prevails is the law of the gun, and within their fiefs the landowners paid scant regard to such official channels for law and order as might exist, dispensing summary justice with the assistance of their henchmen, and enforcing their demands by violent means.

Violence grows easily in the bloodstained soils of Latin America, and its roots are many and varied. One of these roots is the act of colonization. Colonization is an act of violence, whatever well-intentioned colonists may tell you. It is an act of violence because when one people dominates another, they consider their subjects to be inferior and of less worth than themselves.

The first people with whom the Portuguese came into contact were the Indians. The Portuguese saw the Indians as a sickly and lazy people: sickly because they had no resistance to European diseases, and lazy because, being hunter-gatherers, they were unaccustomed to working on the land, and were unwilling to do so.

Having discovered that the Indians made unsatisfactory workers, the Portuguese then imported large numbers of slaves from West Africa, whom they found to be stronger and less able to slip away into the surrounding countryside than the native Indians. But they still thought of them as people of limited understanding, to be treated as children, and punished when they failed to perform as demanded.

Though there was considerable interbreeding among the different groups, it remained the case that the paler the skin, the higher the position in society. Darker skinned people were and still are treated with a mixture of paternalism and authoritarianism that can easily spill over into bully tactics, repression and violence.

The occasional slave rebellion or act of banditry provoked prompt reprisals, and the landowners expected and got support from cash-strapped police who could be hired to deal out justice to the highest bidder. They could also count on the judiciary and the church to support the status quo. In the remoter reaches of the country, this state of affairs continues to this day. It is still common for landowners to hand down their own forms of vigilante justice, employing gunmen for the purpose. As the Parliamentary Commission on the Use of Gunmen (1994) pointed out, "It is cheaper and more efficient to use a gunman than a lawyer." Some landowners still consider themselves to be above the law — viewing themselves much as do gun-toting Westerners in the United States who refuse to pay taxes to support what they see as a corrupt and encroaching system of government.

The primary victims of the landowners' justice are the peasants. Raised to be passive and fatalistic, they struggle to make ends meet under miserable conditions, with minimal health facilities and virtually no education. They have little idea of the rights of citizenship, less still of having human rights. In the face of strong-arm tactics, they find it simpler to give in and move on.

In the far corners of the Amazon, peasant farmers were able, until relatively recently, to live their lives unnoticed and undisturbed. When the government started developing the region by building the first roads, however, the trouble began. Settlers of a different stripe came into the area, and started appropriating the land. And, in the time-honored fashion of the powerful, they met the resistance of those who lived there with violence. The peasants, who little dreamt that things could be otherwise, gave in.

Though they didn't know it, the tide of history was finally beginning to turn in their favor. Their support was to come — of all unexpected places — from the church. Brazilians are a deeply religious people, and although the majority of church authorities were traditionally on the side of the powers-that-be, nevertheless there was a small but increasingly vociferous minority that held the radical view that Christians should seek to do as Christ had done. And what Christ had done had been to work with the outcasts of society: the poor, the disadvantaged, the sick and the women. This new theology encouraged church members to work together with the poor towards a more just and fair society.The greatest need of poor rural dwellers is access to the land, church activists reasoned, and where the peasants are confronted with a group of land grabbers, they must be taught how to resist.

In the face of widespread discontent and the much-touted threat of communism, a military government took over in Brazil in 1964. In order to maintain control, it restricted the right of assembly. But even the military government never quite dared challenge the power of the church, and so church groups (newly christened 'base communities') became the only safe places where people could meet together and plan political action. Church workers began to go out into the rural areas and encourage poor farmers to take charge of their lives and stand up against the violence perpetrated by land-owners and the authorities. This unexpected resistance led to further acts of repression on the part of the landowners; before they realized that circumstances had changed, they had a land war on their hands.

This is the story of one community's struggle for survival, and how its people were affected by one particularly shocking event: the murder of their parish priest.

I was living in the coastal city of Recife when I first heard of the murder of Padre Josimo, but it was to be another seven years before I set out to discover more about his story. What prompted my quest was the realization that there were twelve million people who didn't have enough land to live on, despite the fact that there were millions of acres of land lying unused. I had seen the dispossessed living in their cardboard shacks in the big cities, I knew about the struggle for the land, I had heard that brave souls were living and working in the disputed areas to help landless squatters survive, and I knew that some of them were getting killed. Like Josimo.

So I set off to learn his story. I started by traveling to a place where you can hire a killer for twenty bucks, although I didn't know that at the time. I went to an area called the Parrot's Beak, a place where there have been a hundred and ninety land-related murders in seven years. A hundred and ninety murders, and one conviction.

It doesn't look like a land to die for. It's a flat land by the two great rivers, the Araguaia and the Tocantins, inhabited for centuries by a few scattered groups of Indians, and later by small groups of migrants from the dry lands to the east. Nobody else went there; it was a long way from Brazil's major cities, difficult to get to, and not very rewarding if you succeeded. The few settlers who got there lived near the rivers, and practiced shifting cultivation, planting their crops wherever they pleased. They grew a little manioc, a little rice, a few beans. They hunted and fished, and they made a living. Strictly speaking, they weren't owners, they were squatters. By living and working the land, they did, in fact, acquire squatters' rights under the law. But they didn't know that.

Their ownership of the land wasn't a problem until the 1960s, however, when the Brazilian government suddenly woke up to the fact that half of Brazil was in the Amazon where, beneath the forest floor, all sorts of mineral riches lay buried. In the eyes of the government, the Amazon region was so sparsely inhabited as to be virtually empty — a view, however mistaken, that has not been uncommon to European settler colonists worldwide.* Considerations of sovereignty , security and development demanded that, in the words of the government, this 'land without people' should be

---

* While the present indigenous population in the Amazon can be estimated at some 130,000 people living on a tract of land more than half the size of the continental U.S., earlier estimates of the indigenous population in the 16th-17th centuries numbered it in the millions. As development in the Brazilian interior proceeds and indigenous tribes are threatened with physical and/or cultural extinction, questions concerning their land habitation and ownership may well form an important element among other considerations related to land reform in the region.

given to 'people without land'. Brazilians traditionally cling like limpets to their lovely lazy coastline, so how in the world was the government going to persuade them to brave Amazonian mud and mosquitoes? By offering them land and jobs. Jobs for the starving peasants of the drought-stricken northeast, who would migrate to the Amazon, providing a pool of low-cost labor to build the roads, the dams and the cities that the new frontier would need. And huge expanses of land to set up cattle ranches for the export of beef, thereby transforming what they saw as unproductive forest land into a generator of much-needed foreign currency. It was a program of development geared to the needs of foreign banks, foreign markets, and domestic elites; the price for it would be paid by the great masses of people, and paid all too dearly.

The government sweetened its offer to the ranchers with generous fiscal incentives, tax rebates, negative interest loans, free money of all kinds. And hundreds of them came swarming in to try their luck. The first area of the Amazon they headed for was the land that lay along the brave new highways, Belem-Brasília and the Transamazônica. As fate would have it, the Parrot's Beak lay at the intersection of these two highways, and thus it became the site of the earliest and the dirtiest of the Amazon land wars — wars that continue to this day.

Speculators of all kinds came rushing in: lawyers, doctors, architects, judges, even farmers — all intent on laying their hands on as much land as they possibly could. Nine out of ten of them paid nominal prices for their land and had no intention of making a living out of it — or even living on it. They were holding it as a hedge against inflation, planning to make big money as its value soared. Sometimes, to their annoyance, they found themselves in conflict with a family or two of squatters who laid claim to the same lands. The simplest solution to this was to hire a foreman and give him full license to do whatever might be necessary in order to acquire "clean" title. Then they would serve the peasants with eviction orders, burn them out, terrorize them, sometimes even kill them.

At first, the squatters didn't know what to do. They were simple people. They lived isolated lives, and their main concern was to stay out of trouble. So they would give up their lands, move on, and start over. But then, at the end of the turbulent decade of the seventies, they began to find some support from the Catholic

Church. Inspired by the heady new doctrines of liberation theology, the Brazilian church set up the Pastoral Land Commission (CPT), with the mandate of supporting rural workers, landless peasants and those who worked the land but had no title to it.

"Stay on your lands," the CPT told them, "And together we will fight for your rights. Together we will set up unions, together we will resist, and together we will win."

So the peasants hung on. They learned that by living and working on the lands for a certain period of time, they could acquire squatters' rights which would allow them first some security of tenure, and later the chance to get title to the land. They started to work together, forming associations and unions, and they began to resist the strong-arm tactics of the ranchers, even on occasion meeting gunfire with gunfire. Even more important than what they did was how they felt about themselves. They started thinking of themselves collectively. After years of being kicked in the teeth by the landowners, they suddenly began to stand up for themselves.

This was deeply disturbing to the large landowners, who responded by refining their tactics. In addition to corrupting police and justice officials to the greatest extent possible, they began to hire professional gunmen, and to select their targets with greater care. They focused on union leaders, lawyers, members of the CPT — anyone who was effectively supporting the peasants. They published lists of marked men and women, citing the prices on their heads. They made sure their victims got to hear about it. And when they fired, they seldom missed. On May 10th, 1986, they killed Padre Josimo.

My research for this book began in Rio de Janeiro, in the libraries that document human rights abuses. I spent three months in the field traveling, taping and transcribing interviews. I was helped at every step of the way by the staff of the Pastoral Land Commission who generously provided me with beds, rides, meals, and corners in which to work. Thanks to them, I was introduced to many people who had known Josimo well: his fellow workers and colleagues, church officials, lawyers, community leaders and activists, and the true heroes of the struggle: the squatters themselves.

I also spoke to local officials, police and gunmen. I was unable to interview most of those who had planned the murder and paid the *pistoleiro*, however, because they had long since vanished underground.

Padre Josimo lived and worked in an obscure and distant corner of a vast country that at the time of his death was just beginning to emerge from the twenty year twilight of a military dictatorship. Communications were poor, news was still partially censored, and most of the world at that time considered Brazil (along with the rest of Latin America) to be in a state of intractable chaos, so they paid little attention to it.

Yet when Josimo died at age thirty-three, there were many, active in the field of human rights both inside the country and overseas, who mourned his passing. It is my hope that this book will fill in some of the little known history of a remarkable group of people.

My thanks are due to so many people who helped and encouraged me on this quest: the staff of the CPT, the staff of FASE in Rio, (in particular the librarian, Leonor), Luiza Gardiner who encouraged me throughout, and of course, the people whose names appear in this book.

Padre Josimo Morais Tavares

♦ **Chapter One** ♦

The Priest and the *Pistoleiro*

Everyone knew that Padre Josimo was going to die. The whole town had been talking of nothing else for weeks. Even the mayor had been overheard to say, "We'll have to get rid of that priest, come what may." And since the time when an unknown car had overtaken his on a lonely stretch of road at night and an unknown *pistoleiro* had pumped five bullets into his car door, no doubt Josimo had come to believe it too.

Josimo was facing a hideous dilemma. He didn't want to be killed, yet he couldn't quite bring himself to run away. He knew full well how much the local ranchers detested him for championing the rights of the miserably exploited peasants. When they were evicted from their lands, Josimo supported them and encouraged them to return. He told them about their rights, and helped them set up unions and join the Workers' Party. When the peasants were beaten up, Josimo denounced the ranchers and their strongmen, and complained to the police. He was tireless in the defense of the defenseless. He was a thorn in the side of the landowners, he was a source of considerable annoyance to the police and the local authorities, who considered that he was behaving in a manner most unsuitable to a parish priest. Most infuriating to them, he was a black man. This was the final insult. Josimo's enemies had been gunning for him for some time, but recently they'd been getting too close for comfort.

Saturday, May 10th, 1986 dawned hot and clear. "It was a beautiful day, not a day for terrible things to happen," remarked Perpétua later on.

Inside the parish house in São Sebastião, Padre Josimo slung his leather bag over his shoulder, grabbed a pile of books and adjusted his new straw hat at a becoming angle. Edna, the young catechist, came up behind him humming a few bars from the popular song, "Tall, dark and handsome."

"I've never seen you in a hat before," she remarked. "What's going on?"

"It's so the *pistoleiros* won't recognize me," he grinned and swung out through the kitchen to the yard. The night before, a group of his friends had been sitting around the kitchen table eating potato chips and kidding Josimo about living dangerously.

"Don't worry," he told them half seriously, "If they don't get me when I'm thirty-three, I'll live to be eighty."

It was nine o'clock when Josimo tossed his bags into the back of the blue Toyota.

"OK, Domingos," he said to his bearded assistant. "See you tomorrow."

"Josimo!" His mother, Dona Olinda, frowned sternly up at him. "Aren't you going to take Domingos with you? You know I don't like you traveling alone."

"I'll be fine, mother," Josimo said comfortingly. "I've asked Domingos to take a message to the Sisters. Maybe you'd like to go along too." He knew that Dona Olinda liked nothing better than to visit the French nuns in the next village. Olinda brightened, and with a quick "Be back a week tomorrow," Josimo jumped into the car and was off.

It was nothing new for him to spend more time away than at home; he had a large parish to look after and a lot of traveling to do. Today he was heading eighty miles down the dirt road to Imperatriz, the nearest town of any size, where the Pastoral Land Commission (CPT) had its office. Josimo was the local coordinator, and Imperatriz was where they did their shopping, collected their mail and made their telephone calls. A careful driver, Josimo rounded the corner of the square, waving at a bunch of women there, then headed off on the long bumpy road to Imperatriz.

"Domingos, I wish you had gone with him. You know I don't like him to travel alone," Dona Olinda grumbled.

"I'll be seeing him tomorrow in Tocantinópolis," Domingos said, humoring her. "Come on now, hop in." Off they went in a cloud of dust.

One of the women who had waved at Josimo watched the two cars leave, and hurried to the public telephone. She put through a call to the next village, Augustinópolis. "The man has left," she said, and put down the phone.

Shortly after nine o'clock, gunman Geraldo was downing black coffee and Coca Cola in a bakery in Imperatriz. He was attempting to shift his hangover, and waiting for his orders to come through from Augustinópolis. He'd been offered fifty thousand cruzeiros ($1,750) for the job. They'd warned him he'd better not bungle the job this time around...

In Augustinópolis, town councilor Nenem was preparing a massive barbecue for the seventy military policemen in town. They had come to collect the body of his brother, a much-feared gunman known as Donda. Donda was notorious for his ungovernable temper; when the mood was on him he would shoot anyone who crossed him. He had recently been working as foreman on one of the local farms, and had treated the workers so outrageously that accumulated resentments had finally boiled over. The workers had ambushed Donda and killed him. Not only that, but they had refused to allow the family to collect the body. "Let the dogs eat it," was the message they sent. "That's what Donda used to say when he shot someone."

Nenem's first attempt to retrieve his brother's body was met by a hail of bullets, forcing him to withdraw. He went to the police station for help, and the police chief sent for reinforcements. Seventy military policemen were dispatched for the job, as well as a helicopter. Nothing like this had ever been seen in Augustinópolis, and the town was in a ferment of excitement, with rumors flying in all directions. "It's all the fault of that communist priest," some people were saying. "This sort of thing never used to happen before he came here. Those church people are nothing but a bunch of agitators."

As Josimo approached Augustinópolis, he remembered his friends' repeated warnings: "For God's sake, drive through that place without stopping — it's a hornet's nest if ever there was one." Augustinópolis was the seat of the local ranchers' association, sworn enemy to Josimo and the CPT. Josimo and his friends were fully aware of this, and they knew too that in this town, there were gunmen for hire on every street corner. But as luck would have it, the only road passed through the center of town, and even amid all the excitement, Josimo's distinctive blue Toyota did not pass unnoticed. Nenem was chewing on a chicken bone, while his brother Guiomar opened another bottle of beer. Guiomar gestured toward

Josimo's car and muttered, "There goes a dead man." Brother-in-law Vilson grinned at the other two, tossed his cigarette end onto the ground, and climbed into a yellow car that was waiting in the drive. He slammed his foot to the floor and headed for the open road, overtaking Josimo on the edge of town. Adstonir Resende, head of the ranchers' association, noticed the two cars with great satisfaction. He walked in a leisurely fashion to the public telephone and dialed a number in Imperatriz. "The man has left," he said. A woman took the call the other end. She hurried down to the corner bakery and whispered into the ear of Geraldo, the gunman. Geraldo downed his soda and headed out.

Josimo drove along the dusty road, glad to be past the spot where he had been ambushed not three weeks earlier. This day, there was no hurry. His plan was to leave the Toyota in Imperatriz at the workshop. Later in the day, he would take the bus to Tocantinópolis, at the request of the bishop. He knew just what Dom Aloísio would say. A cautious man, he would advise Josimo to leave the area for a time, arguing that things were getting too hot, and it was time to leave.

The friendly village of São Miguel came into sight. Josimo pulled in at the house of Dona Raimunda Bezerra, one of his staunchest allies and a pillar of the local workers' association. As usual, she rushed out to greet him. She had a document for him to study, and her habitual scolding to administer. "How many times have I told you, Padre Josimo, that you shouldn't be traveling alone?" she demanded. "I'm always uneasy about you crossing that ferry, and that's the truth."

Josimo smiled affectionately at her, and before she could continue, he was saved by the arrival of a young police recruit, football boots in hand, wanting a lift to the Saturday game at the police station by the ferry. A young woman ran up, asking for a ride for herself and three small children, and Josimo packed them all into the back. Straightening his new straw hat, he gave Raimunda a friendly wave, and drove off.

The ferry was always a bottleneck, and the ferry landing a good place for an ambush, with its maze of little wooden huts and tortuous paths. But this day was such a beautiful day, hot and sunny. Tomorrow would be Mother's Day, and Josimo would meet his friends to go off to a meeting down in the south of the state. He could feel the tension draining out of him at the thought of it. He drove onto the ferry and parked his car in the space behind Vilson's. Vilson saw him in his rear-view mirror but made no sign. As the ferry drew in, Vilson was first off the ramp, and disappeared into the maelstrom of people in the narrow street. Josimo followed him slowly, careful not to splash the large crowd

Meanwhile, Geraldo had sobered up, collected his 7.65 mm pistol and stuffed it into his belt. Vilson and he were approaching the CPT office on Avenida Dorgival Pinheiro when they saw the blue Toyota coming towards them. Josimo had dropped off his passengers and was alone. Vilson stopped his car outside the barbecue stand; Geraldo crossed the street and dodged into the copy shop, two doors down from Josimo's office.

Josimo parked the car and hurried up the first flight of steps. He was just turning the corner when he heard someone shout his name. "Ei! Padre Josimo!" He turned and looked back. Below him stood a blond man with long hair, wrestling with something in the waistband of his pants. In a flash, Josimo realized he was pulling a gun, and turned to run. Geraldo fired twice, hitting Josimo in the kidney.

Josimo was dead, but he didn't know it.

◆ Chapter Two ◆

Seeking Josimo in the Back of Beyond

It was February, 1993. I had taken the first step on the trail of Padre Josimo, a trail which would eventually lead me to the infamous Parrot's Beak at the edge of the Amazonian rain forest, where the world's last great land grab is still going on. I was sitting in a lawyer's office in Brasília learning about the time Josimo ran into trouble with the law concerning the destruction of the telephone exchange.

"It was a put up job, of course," said the lawyer, peering at me through her pebble lenses. "They brought a case against him for willful destruction of state property. Never proved a thing, but the case still drags on, believe it or not. Of course, Josimo's been dead for years, but some of his colleagues in the CPT were indicted. In fact," she sniffed indignantly, "There's a hearing scheduled for Tuesday in Itaguatins."

She pointed to the wall map. I could barely see Itaguatins written in very small print at the northern end of the state of Tocantins, a thousand miles from where we sat. "Why don't you come along?" said the lawyer comfortably. "I'll be there, and I can introduce you to some of the characters in the story."

I sailed out of the office in a happy haze. It was Friday afternoon, and it would take me a good twenty-four hours — maybe longer — to get to Itaguatins. With luck, I'd be able to make it in time, and I'd certainly meet some of Josimo's friends. Some of his enemies too, no doubt. Perfect.

A twelve hour bus journey over a bumpy road that had once been paved took me to the town of Gurupi, halfway into the state of Tocantins. I was directed to the small, airless office of the Pastoral Land Commission to talk to one of their lawyers, Adilar.

"Tell me about the CPT," I began. "What is it that you do that makes you so many enemies?"

Adilar poured us both a cup of strong dark coffee, and leaned back in his chair. "Well," he smiled, "I guess it's because we get ourselves involved in the land wars. We see our job as supporting the peasants in every way we can. They don't have title to the land, you see. They never knew such a thing existed. It didn't matter until the great land rush was on, and all of a sudden they found themselves served with eviction orders. Well, the law says they can acquire squatters' rights under certain circumstances, and most of them had a far stronger claim to the land than the big ranchers who got their titles by all sorts of dubious means. Of course, the ranchers do everything in their power to throw the peasants off the land, and that's where we come in, make as much noise as possible, and see if we can establish their tenure. And that's only a first step. Then we've got to figure out ways they can stay on the land. There's no infrastructure at all; no roads, no credit, no nothing. No technology, no marketing, no access to seeds or fertilizer, no help of any sort from anybody. We do what we can to set up cooperatives and credit schemes, and give a little technical advice. So as you can imagine, we make ourselves pretty unpopular among the ranchers. They reckon we're inciting the peasants to revolution, I suppose. That's why we make so many enemies. Now tell me something: which court hearing did you say you were going to attend?"

"Something to do with the destruction of public property," I ventured.

"The case of the telephone exchange?" He snorted. "Let me tell you about that. It was pure fabrication from start to finish. You know that Josimo lived in a little place called São Sebastião? The mayor there was called Zé Carneiro, and if there was one person Zé Carneiro couldn't abide, it was Josimo. I think he thought that Josimo was trying to build a power base, but he couldn't have been more wrong. Anyway, there's another little village up there called Buriti, and the people of Buriti finally got some money from the state to put in a public telephone. Nobody had any quarrel with that, except when the mayor started to build the telephone exchange on a piece of land belonging to the church.

"There was no end of a row about it. Josimo protested to the mayor that it was church land, and asked him to stop construction, but the mayor refused. He even put a guard on the building site. Well, it so happened that Josimo had to be out of town for a couple of weeks, and by the time he came back, the construction was almost complete. The villagers sent him an urgent message asking him to do something, but Josimo realized the mayor wouldn't listen to him.

He suggested they call in the bishop to arbitrate, but the truth was that the people didn't really trust the bishop. They thought he'd sell them down the river. So one dark night, they went in there and knocked the building down. Josimo wasn't actually present, although I'm pretty sure he knew about it.

"The mayor was livid with rage. He called in the police, and they arrested a whole bunch of people and beat the daylights out of them. They managed to line up some witnesses to testify that Josimo and three of the nuns had been in charge of the whole operation — carrying machine guns if you please! The whole thing was one big lie from start to finish. Even the witnesses admitted it was hearsay. The French Sisters were at home twenty miles away, and Josimo kept his head down that night, never stirring out of the place he was staying.

"There's one thing you have to realize in connection with all this. That whole area was under the jurisdiction of the National Security Laws at the time because of the so-called guerrilla war they'd had there in the early '70s. The military government regarded the Araguaia/Tocantins corridor as a flash point for insurrection, so they put it under military law. The whole business of the telephone exchange was blown up into an attack on National Security, exacerbated by the fact that the Sisters are foreigners. The case is still going on, even though Josimo's out of it, of course. The whole thing's a complete farce. It'll give you a good insight into Brazilian justice."

That evening, I marched across town to the bus station and found a bus heading for Araguaina. "Should get in around 0300," said the driver. "You can pick up another bus from there." Long experience had taught me how to arrange self, pack, water bottle, sweater and legs to best advantage, and I settled down to doze my way along the bumpy Belem-Brasília highway.

At 3:00 a.m., we arrived at the dark and cheerless bus station in Araguaina. There was no bus waiting. I stared disbelievingly at a wooden board on which was painted the time of the next bus to Itaguatins: 14:00 hrs. Eleven hours to wait. It was not an encouraging thought.

I sat down to consider my position. A small child materialized out of the shadows and began tugging insistently at my arm.

"There's someone who wants to see you," he whispered.

I didn't like the sound of that, either.

But the someone proved to be the driver of an ancient and decrepit bus called JAMJOY.

"Itaguatins?" he inquired brightly. "Come with me and I'll drop you at Estreita. There'll be a connecting bus waiting." It sounded unlikely, but a lot better than sitting in Araguaina. I fought my way to the last seat, well to the rear of the bus. It looked as if the bus had been on the road for several days. There was a thick layer of garbage on the floor and it had a homely lived-in smell. Luckily no-one had been throwing up lately.

It was still dark when we got to Estreita. There was nothing there at all — just a muddy little intersection, and predictably, no sign of the promised bus. I could see no advantage in staying at Estreita; better, I decided, to throw in my lot with my fellow passengers. At the next town, the driver suggested off-loading me and several others. "You take a canoe across the river and walk up to the bus station," he suggested. "You can get a bus to Itaguatins from there."

"The bus doesn't run any more," objected one of the passengers.

"There's sure to be a truck," said the driver cheerfully.

That idea had no appeal. It seemed altogether better to stick it out until we reached Imperatriz and start over from there. At least it would be daylight. I settled myself in as best I could and dozed fitfully as far as Imperatriz.

The bus station was ankle deep in garbage, and there were muddy puddles everywhere. I seized my pack and headed off into the humid heat of the morning. The bus driver pointed to an even older and muddier JAMJOY bus which was just on the point of pulling out. "That's your bus," he said, thumping on the side of it. "Get off in Sítio Novo and you can hitch a ride from there."

I scrambled aboard the bus, picking my way carefully over sacks and bundles which were piled up just inside the door. The bus rattled its way down to the river bank, and the passengers piled out into the mud. I trudged onto the ferry and staked out a seat next to an overweight Bolivian who told me that he was a bush pilot working in the gold mines of the interior. "I fly out the gold," he told me confidentially. "And on the return journey," he tapped the side of his nose and looked at me significantly, "I bring in the women."

The ferry pulled in, disgorging several pickups, a couple of horse carts, a host of muddy passengers and the JAMJOY bus. We picked our way across the puddles and settled back in our lumpy seats. I lay back and gazed through the dirty windows at the strip of land known as the Parrot's Beak, the land that Josimo had died for.

The Parrot's Beak lies between the Araguaia and the Tocantins, two of the large rivers that make up the Amazon river system. Innocent green palm trees cover one of the most violent and bloody regions of a violent continent. The violence and the bloodshed are caused by wars over ownership of the land.

In the beginning, no one bothered to lay claim to the land. Land was regarded as a gift from God, something to be used, not to be owned. All that changed in 1960, when the federal government put in the first road. Before that, the region had been inhabited by small bands of Indians and others of mixed European and African descent who had drifted in by river, attracted by fertile lands, or the occasional find of gold or diamonds. To the east lie the great drylands of Piauí, Ceará and Maranhão, which have always provided and still provide a steady stream of migrants heading west to the green lands by the great rivers. The early settlers cleared patches of forest and put in their little fields of manioc, rice, beans and corn. They built small settlements and named them after the first arrivals: Firmino's Center, Ferreiro's Center, Center of the Mulattos. The fields were moved every year or two, for there was land enough for everyone. Babassu palm trees grew in profusion, and the women pressed delicious cooking oil from the nuts, wove baskets from the leaves, and made charcoal from the husks. There were fish in the rivers and game in the forest. The land provided a good living for those who didn't need to plan very far ahead. Although no one had title to the land, they were entitled by law to squatters' rights. They never knew about that until it was too late.

The Parrot's Beak — so named for its shape on the map — lies at the extreme northern end of the state of Tocantins, which split off from Goiás in 1988. It is more than a thousand miles north of the federal capital, Brasília. One of the chief reasons for building Brasília was to attract development to the hitherto untouched heartland of continent-sized Brazil, and in order to do this it was necessary to build some roads. The very first of these, the Road of the Jaguar, was scheduled to cut across the eastern edge of Amazonia to the mouth of the Amazon river at Belem.

Construction began in 1960. For the inhabitants of the Parrot's Beak, the good times vanished like the morning mist. People came swarming up the new road looking for land, looking for gold, looking for a new life. Since the peasants had no clear understanding of the concept of property, they were easily persuaded to part from their lands in exchange for a rifle, a bicycle, or a piece of paper promising some money.

The new owners started to fence off the land, and forbade access to the babassu palm trees. They moved in, announced that the land was now theirs, and produced documents to prove it. Any families in residence were ordered to leave, and those who protested soon attracted unwelcome attention from hired gunmen. If that didn't frighten them off, they were served with eviction notices. Entire villages were emptied, houses and crops were burnt, and the people were intimidated, beaten up and sometimes killed. In their bewilderment, they found no place to turn.

But help was at hand. In 1979, a lay missionary from Italy arrived in the Parrot's Beak. His name was Nicola. He started walking from community to community, listening to the problems of the peasants, advising them of their legal rights, and helping them organize the first elements of resistance. He was joined soon afterwards by three French nuns, Mada, Bia, and Nicole, and a Brazilian nun called Lurdinha, from the far south of the country. In 1983, Padre Josimo came to take over the parish of São Sebastião, a small village right at the end of the Parrot's Beak. For a short time, this extraordinarily talented and courageous group was to challenge the power of the establishment, stand up for the dispossessed, and threaten the local power structure. It was to be a long hard battle, and Josimo was to pay for it with his life.

This was the story I had come in search of, and as I looked at the faces of my fellow passengers on the bus, I tried to imagine which of them had known Josimo, and what effect he had had on their lives.

The stony road managed to be both muddy and dusty at the same time. We were traveling through a green landscape: low forest, lots of babassu palms, small clearings of corn, beans, rice, and manioc, and the occasional cattle pastures. The villages are nothing but higgledy-piggledy collections of mud huts with thatch roofs, but Sítio Novo has turned itself into a town and boasts a large square, a telephone office, and several paved roads.

The local office of the Pastoral Land Commission is just off the main square, next to the church. I wandered over to check whether Xavier, the French Dominican friar who was setting up lines of credit for the local village associations, was home. But the office was all shut up. I stuck a note under the door and made my way back to the square in the hope of finding a ride to Itaguatins. Several pickup trucks were parked there, but they were all going the other way. Itaguatins, it seems, was on the road to nowhere. "Best thing is to go wait at the turnoff," advised one of the villagers. "Most of the traffic going through here is headed for Imperatriz."

I shouldered my pack and headed for the turnoff. Fortunately there was a house there, and better still, the ancient owner invited me into the shade, where there was a rocking chair strung with broken plastic. All the traffic, without exception, was going to Imperatriz. The old man got bored of talking to me and went inside to take a siesta. His rhythmic snores filled me with an overwhelming desire to do the same, but the confines of the plastic rocking chair did not permit.

It was one o'clock, the hearing was scheduled for two thirty, and there seemed to be no way I could get there on time. I was beginning to get a bit edgy when a telephone company truck drew up in a cloud of dust and I caught a ride. By a miracle, we arrived in Itaguatins by two. I did not find the bustle I had expected to see, with lawyers swarming all over the place. The town was wrapped in profound silence. I made my way to the Forum and inquired. "Hearing?" yawned the girl at the desk as she listlessly pecked at an elderly typewriter. "Oh no, it's been canceled. The judge is on holiday."

I flounced out and looked venomously at the small town. It consisted of two streets of neatly painted houses. Very small donkeys wandered around. The flooded brown river swept past. Everyone was asleep. I sought refuge in the priest's house. Even though he was traveling, I was welcome to stay the night. There was no bus before the morning. I dumped my stuff and whiled away the rest of the day listening to one of the justice officials telling me about his blameless part in the local land evictions. We both knew he was lying. It was almost too hot to matter. But he did mention, in passing, that there were a couple of murders out in Mata Seca a short time back.

After a restless and mosquito-ridden night, I was up at dawn to catch the bus to Itaguatins. I heard the sound of a car engine approaching, and to my immense delight, who should round the corner but Xavier, the French friar from Sitio Novo, together with a jeepload of people from the Rural Workers' Union. They were heading for Mata Seca to check out the murders.

In response to my urgent request, Xavier decided he could squeeze in one more. This was far better than attending an audience at the forum. Right there were three of the best-known figures of the whole land struggle in the area: Dona Raimunda, who once lunched with Danielle Mitterrand in Paris — and didn't think much of the food; João Custódio, veteran of innumerable standoffs with the police; and Maria Senhora, the articulate black union leader from the Centro dos Mulatos. Together with Xavier, his colleague Pedro, and a couple of other union officials, we were to spend the next forty-eight hours in Mata Seca, hearing the full story of the murders, and helping the squatters draw up a plan of action. These were the first land-related deaths in this particular area, and the squatters had sent out an urgent plea for help.

"Hey!" shouted Pedro, wrestling with the steering wheel as the Toyota bucked across the ruts. "Tell us the story of Mata Seca, somebody."

"It's a complex situation," said Iran, the union leader from Tocantinópolis. "To start with, Mata Seca is Indian land, although the Apinajá have never objected to the squatters. There are sixteen squatter families there, and most of them have lived on their own little plots for more than fifteen years without any problems. Then this guy Gideão shows up and says he has title to a piece of land in the middle, right next to Zé Barros and Mauro. At first, he doesn't bother them. But then he decides he likes the look of their lands, so he hires a *pistoleiro* to go round scaring them off. The first thing that happens is that Zé Barros' house gets burned down. Luckily there's no one in it. Then they set fire to his corn crop. Fifteen acres of it.

Then this same *pistoleiro*, Gerínio, son of Rattlesnake, goes over to Mauro's place and starts shooting at the fence posts. These were only intimidation tactics, of course, but pretty effective all the same. So the squatters get together and go talk to the police about it, and eventually seven families sign a good neighbor statement with Gideão.

"But it doesn't end there. One day, Zé Barros and one of his sons — a young lad of fifteen or so — are out in the field and they hear that the *pistoleiro*, Gerínio, is around. They hide in their little shelter, and when Gerínio comes along, Zé Barros plugs him with his shotgun. What Zé Barros doesn't see is that Gideão's son, Gidevan, is right behind him, and when Zé stands up to take a look, Gidevan shoots him dead. Zé Barros just has time to shout to his boy, who takes a shot at Gidevan. Fortunately, he misses.

"Rumor has it Gideão has hired a whole lot more gunmen, and he's as mad as a snake because they had a go at his son. Half of the squatters are in fear and trembling and the other half are hell-bent on revenge. If you ask me, I'd say the thing could blow up any time."

I closed my eyes and wondered what I was getting myself into, simply by seeking to write about Josimo. I'd known what was going on in the Amazon land wars. I'd actually volunteered to come to the Amazon and investigate them, triggered by the figure of twelve million landless peasants in a land the size of the United States. Twelve million people forced to take to the road in search of a living. It was as if the entire population of Calcutta had packed up its bags and bundles and was off to find a new life. I knew that hundreds of thousands of families had been trapped in the cruel cardboard slums of the huge cities, others had drifted into poorly paid jobs in construction and industry, while still others had succumbed to gold fever and rushed like lemmings to the subhuman conditions of the gold mines. And countless thousands had swarmed to the agricultural frontier as it swept into the sparsely populated spaces of Amazonia, where they had cleared their patches of forest, planted their crops, and watched their dreams die as the soils were exhausted. I had spoken to families who had doggedly moved on -- five, ten times, leaving their lands to be snapped up by the wave of speculators that followed them like a pack of hyenas.

But I could sense that here in Mata Seca things were different. The people here were making a stand. They had found fertile lands at last, they had raised their crops, and they intended to stay put.

In addition to the local ranchers, the squatters were facing other forces beyond their ken that were equally determined to move them on. Nine out of ten squatters had never heard of the Greater Carajás Project, the multi-billion dollar scheme to develop one of the richest mineral areas in the world. But they all knew about the gold strike at Serra Pelada; most families had at least one member who had tried his luck there at one time or another. What they didn't know was that, as part of the Greater Carajás Project, government planners had zoned their area for cattle ranching. The idea was to raise beef for export and send it out on the Carajás railroad to the port at São Luis. On a still night, the inhabitants of São Sebastião could hear the train whistle as it passed by on the other side of the river, but they were completely unaware of the implications of the government's mammoth development plan. Cattle ranching requires capital, and it requires large stretches of land. Cattle ranching is inimical to small squatters on subsistence plots, and that is why the government had given its tacit consent to their expulsion. There were only two organizations fighting for the dispossessed: the church and the unions. Without support from these, the squatters would have been wiped out.

After several wrong turns, we arrived at a clearing in the forest and parked the car in front of a small house of wooden stakes with a thatch roof, the house of Mazoniel, head of the recently formed squatters' association. During the course of the morning, several squatters drifted in, and finally the meeting got under way. The men were thin, sharp-faced, watchful as a pack of wolves. Each one propped his rifle up against the wall within easy reach. We sat on benches made of tree trunks, ranged round the wall. The women huddled in the kitchen. One or two small children and dogs played on the beaten earth floor. There was a table, a shelf with a water filter, a few posters on the walls. The bedroom was half partitioned off and next to it was the kitchen, with its mud stove and its shelves full of plates and mugs. A stout board outside held a tin wash-pan and the gourd of washing-up water. Bathing was done in the river. Anything else in the forest.

The squatters reconstructed the story for us. They were jittery, expecting more violence. There was a stir when one-eyed Mauro came in; he had come out of hiding for the occasion. The tension was cut by the calm voice of João Custódio, speaking from his long experience. He explained that the trick is for people to stay together. To work together. One man makes an easy target, but a gunman won't take on a group. If people stick together, they won't get killed. The men eyed one another uneasily. Dona Raimunda marched into the centre of the room and, looking over her glasses, she addressed them as if they were a bunch of unruly schoolchildren. She bent over to draw a triangle on the dirt floor.

"This," she announced, "is called a pyramid. It shows us how the world works. At the top here, the pointed bit, are the very few people who live at the expense of all the others at the bottom. Deep down, we all want to be at the top. But we can only climb up by treading on our companions. And if we do that, we'll be on our own.

"Do you know something? We human beings aren't nearly as smart as the animals. They know they can't be safe if they're alone. They know they need to be together; they do it by instinct. But we keep wanting to do things by ourselves. That's why people don't join the union," she looked round fiercely, "because they can't see what's in it for them. I tell you what's in it: if we're all together we can get what we want. If we try on our own, we'll never get anywhere."

Maria Senhora was soft-spoken but firm, not the combative type. "What we have to remember about the union is this," she began. "It doesn't matter how few you are, so long as you all act together. Let me tell you the story of Zé Antônio. The ranchers came to him and said they wanted his land. They even said they'd compensate him. Then they looked a little closer and saw that Zé Antônio had a lot of fruit trees, so they'd have to pay a lot more than they'd planned. They sent round a *pistoleiro* to see the lie of the land. Pretended he wanted to buy some chickens. Well, Zé didn't like the look of the *pistoleiro* so he told him to come back in the morning and the chickens would be ready. Meantime he sent for all his friends. Next morning, they were all waiting when the *pistoleiro* came and they caught him and made him confess. Well, if they hadn't gotten together and made a plan, someone would have been killed. Anyone can see that."

"I use the picture of the swarm of bees," said Mazoniel. "Mess about with one and the rest will be after you."

"Right!" said Raimunda. "That's why you must move your houses. Build them close together. Put them so close you can smell each other's food cooking. You never know when you're going to need each other. The *pistoleiros* won't go after you if you're all together, but if you're alone they'll pick you off one by one."

The squatters discussed the matter over lunch, bowls of rice and beans with roasted manioc. Halfway through the meal there was a commotion as three strangers rode up. Mauro slipped into the kitchen, and four or five of the men picked up their rifles and went outside. Through the wooden stockade walls we could see the strangers approach. One of them took out a bottle of the local firewater and passed it round. There was a short, stilted conversation, and they turned to leave. No sooner were they out of sight than Raimunda laid into the men. "I don't know what you boys were thinking of!" she harangued them. "Accepting a nip out of the bottle like that! Anybody'd think you were born yesterday. I suppose they asked you your names?" Bashful silence and averted eyes confirmed her suspicion. "You never do that again, do you hear me? They're only trying to find out who's here. Looking for Mauro, I don't doubt." Mauro shrank into his corner. He was blind in one eye. I felt heart sore for him.

Later that evening, I talked to Dona Antonia, Zé Barros' widow. A frail woman, she was still in shock.

"We'd been married thirty years," she whispered. "Zé Barros was as good a man as you'll find. Never harmed a fly. And here am I with seven children and no food in the house. I haven't had the nerve to set foot in the fields since that day." Her ravaged face bore eloquent testimony to her suffering.

"Never harmed a fly." The thought haunted me as I lay in my hammock that night. We strung our hammocks in a row, and I put mine well in the middle, convincing myself that Raimunda was right and there would be no shoot-out tonight because we were all together. Zé Barros never harmed a fly. But he killed the *pistoleiro*. Had it been just like killing a snake, something done on the spur of the moment? Had he planned it? My thoughts whirled round and round. THOU SHALT NOT KILL. What, then, shall we do?

Chapter Three

"I want to be a priest"

I went to the village of Sampaio to visit Josimo's mother, Dona Olinda. A small, timid woman with a worn face, she received me shyly and courteously.

"Josimo always knew what he wanted," she told me in her soft voice. "'It's no good, Mother,' he said to me. 'I know you want me to work in the fields. But that's not what I want. I want to be a priest.'"

"Tell me about it," I prompted her.

"I was fourteen years old when Josimo was born," she continued. "It was Easter Saturday, 1953. We lived in Marabá, over in Pará. I was washing clothes by the banks of the Araguaia river and when the pains started, there wasn't time to get back to the house. I had the baby right there, by the river. My husband wasn't there. He used to go away for weeks at a time, and it was the neighbors who helped me with the child, and my mother. Not my real mother, but the woman who raised me.

"My husband got himself another woman when Josimo was two, and by that time I had another child. So I took the children and I moved to Xambioá. I didn't know anyone there, but God gave me courage. I used to wash clothes and cook. I didn't want to marry again, in case my husband beat the children.

"Josimo was desperate to study. He couldn't wait to get to school. But when he got there, the teacher used to beat him and he used to come home crying. So I took him out. Then they started a parish school. I said he couldn't go because he wasn't old enough. But the nuns came to see me and told me I ought to let him go. In the end, I did. When he was in his third year, they made a list of those students who wanted to go to seminary. Naturally, Josimo wanted to go. He put his name on the list without telling me. One day he said to me, 'Mother, I have to tell you something. I've put my name down for seminary. I want to go with my friends.'

"Padre Joâo and Dom Cornélio, our bishop, were behind it. I fought with them about it. I said Josimo was too little, but the bishop said, 'The boy has a vocation.' I said, 'No, I won't let him go, he's too small. Hardly eleven years old.' Well, those two kept coming round and pestering me. One day they arrived at five in the morning and said, 'Look, we've got a bag here with all the clothes he'll need, and a towel and everything.' Josimo said, 'Yes, yes, I want to go,' and the padre said, 'I'll take care of everything. I'll pay for him for three years.'

"'The boy is mine,' I said, 'I won't let you take him away.' And I started to cry. Then Padre Joâo said to me, 'Don't cry. It's only Tocantinópolis. He'll send you letters so you'll hear how he is getting on, and I'll bring him back to see you.' But I still wouldn't let him go.

"Josimo cried and cried, and spent the whole day in bed. He wouldn't eat anything. In the end, he went to a neighbor and told her he wanted to go to seminary but I wouldn't let him. He asked her if it would be a sin to run away, and she said it wouldn't, because he had a vocation. She told him she'd come and talk to me.

"When he left, it was worse than if he had died."

I went to Tocantinópolis to take a look at the seminary Josimo had attended as a boy. I was warmly welcomed by a band of cleaning ladies energetically mopping the spotless floors. The place smelled of disinfectant.

"How do you like our seminary?" they asked, showing me classroom after identical classroom, desks lined up with military precision, the only decoration a large crucifix in each room. I thought of young Josimo, barely eleven years old. It must have been a rigorous education.

I talked to Padre Carmelo, seminary director. "I wasn't here in Josimo's time," he told me. "But I got to know him later, when he was a priest.

"He stayed in Tocantinópolis, probably until he was 14 or 15. He received a very traditional education here, extremely strict. It laid a good foundation, but nowadays we find it too hard on the boys. In later years, Josimo felt he'd been deprived of affection, and I'm sure he was right.

"He felt, too, the lack of a father figure. Over the course of his schooling, he attached himself more and more to Dom Cornélio, the bishop in charge of his education. Ten years after first leaving home for seminary, he broke out of his former reticence and sent Dom Cornélio this letter, dated July 29th 1974:

> I loved your letter of April 8th. Especially the last part. It brings me to a point I've been wanting to reach for a long time, the stage of being able to share my problems with you. I've never found an opportunity before now. What can have happened? Was it my fault? Your fault? My shyness?
>
> I see in this openness of yours a way for two people to meet, to get to know each other. It's something we need to do. It's the only way that our work will bear fruit. Let's work together. Let's not be strangers any more. Fellow workers need to love each other. To love each other, we need to know each other. This requires effort on both our parts. We both have to be open to each other. We have to recognize the positive sides of one another. Know what each of us is capable of. I'm ready to do this. I'm ready to open myself to you. Ask me if you want to know something about me. Help me to let you know me better.

Padre Carmelo glanced up. "Later in the letter, he comes back to his relationship with the bishop." He read on:

> I trust in you. You've been very good to me. Yet, forgive me, but I see your generosity as something distant. You send me to one seminary or another. You pay for everything, and I'm truly grateful. But I don't find a warm relationship between us. Two people who love each other. It's not that I doubt your friendship. You told me in your last letter that I was the apple of your eye. But I'd like us to be closer. To be able to talk. About ourselves. I'd like to be able to talk about myself. And I don't think our relationship is one of two friends who talk to each other. Please don't take offense at this. I'm not blaming you. I'm just trying to get it right.

From Tocantinópolis, Josimo had moved to Brasília, and then to Aparecida do Norte in the state of São Paulo. After studying philosophy and literature, he went to Petrópolis to attend the Franciscan Seminary. One of his teachers was Leonardo Boff, the apostle of Liberation Theology. Brother Leonardo did not remember Josimo as being anything out of the ordinary. "He was a good student," he said. "Very quiet and even tempered. He wasn't a leader. But he was decisive. He made up his mind to work for the poor, and never wavered."

"Those were the great days of Liberation Theology," said Padre Carmelo. "It might have been tailor-made for Josimo. He knew what it was all about. You must remember that he was black. He was teased a lot about that, but he never minded. He was also extremely poor. He had no father, his mother was illiterate, and his only sister died of malnutrition. So this new theology was a revelation to him."

The great cry of Liberation Theologians echoes the cry raised in the Old Testament, "Let my people go." Free them from the domination of the rich and powerful, free them from the power structure of the church itself. Jehovah demands justice, not sacrifice. Jesus preaches the Kingdom of God on earth as well as in heaven, brought about through the dedication of God's people. Inspired by the Holy Spirit, God's people are to live in community, seeking justice, righteousness and peace. Their manual is the Bible, and their goal is to live lives modeled on the life of Christ, offering succor, sustenance, and above all, justice, to the poor and oppressed.

Heady stuff, and deeply threatening to those in authority. Poor, black, and a child of peasant stock, Josimo knew all about repression and discrimination. His childhood home, Xambioá, had been the center of a small but determined guerrilla movement in the early 1970s, which had been violently put down by the army. As for discrimination, a black man would have met that often enough, even in Brazil, a country that prides itself on its harmonious race relations and turns a blind eye to the realities: the darker the skin, the lower the status. Yet, instead of using the priesthood as a means of social advancement and turning his back on his humble origins, Josimo was determined to go home and live out his Christian life to the full.

"He was an extraordinary communicator," Padre Carmelo said. "He wasn't just an intellectual theologian. He was able to interpret his culture to his parishioners and theirs to us. He could talk to the people and understand them, and he was able to see and respond to their needs. His whole life was a logical consequence of the choices he made. He was completely committed to living out the Gospel. So he took upon himself a whole series of problems: social problems, family problems, all the tensions and challenges of the region. He learned to balance faith and life, politics and reality, in a manner from which there was no turning back."

Josimo wrote to the bishop on April 30th, 1974:

> I don't want to be an priest who stays all the time in his study,
> and I don't want to be an ignoramus. I'd like to be as well-read as
> a theologian, yet simple and humble enough to work with the
> people.

He saw his role as threefold: he must be a pastor, a prophet
and a priest. He should live simply among the poor, sharing their
struggles and bringing them the presence of God in the midst of
violence and inhumanity. He should help them to unite, so that
together they could work to transform their daily life. He should be
courageous and unwavering, denouncing injustice and awakening
hope in the midst of crisis.

As the date of his ordination approached, Josimo sent out
invitations in the form of an exuberant poem.

> To be a priest
> is to feel life
> springing forth;
> rendering service
> to God and to the poor
> above all.
>
> The justice of God
> is like the wind;
> either it blows gently
> like a breeze,
> or it explodes
> like a tempest!
>
> It is pleasing to God
> to serve the poor
> the sick,
> those on the edges of life.
>
> To be a priest
> is to seek to live
> the life of Christ
> through the strength
> of communal love.
>
> A padre is
> a prophet in justice,

a pastor on the journey
a humble priest
who seeks
to offer
righteous offerings
to God!

Josimo was ordained by his mentor, Dom Cornélio, on January 20th, 1979, and went to live in the parish of Wanderlândia, not many miles from his childhood home of Xambioá. Here he worked with Padre Atílio, an Italian priest once anonymously described as "a left-wing agitator who influences the people against the government, the large landowners, and the laws of the land." Shortly after Josimo's arrival, Padre Atílio left the parish and Josimo was on his own.

He had a lot on his plate. He worked in the high school and undertook the pastoral care of the diocesan youth. He quickly understood that the most urgent problem facing his parishioners was the question of the land. It was a subject on which he had strong views. He reckoned that land existed to sustain people, and that everyone had the right to as much land as he needed to support his family. He lost no opportunity to denounce the land-grabbers, and earned himself such hostility that he began to receive death threats. The police told him to keep out of it, otherwise he might end up in jail, like the two French padres from São Geraldo. As the land situation deteriorated and evictions, burnings and torture increased, Josimo volunteered to work in the Pastoral Land Commission. This job was such a hot potato that the bishop had to appeal repeatedly for volunteers, and even Josimo hesitated before committing himself to the job that would lead to his death.

But that all lay in the future. I wanted to find out more about Josimo's early days as a priest. In Tocantinópolis, seat of the diocese, I met Padre Mariano, who turned out to be an unconditional fan of Josimo's. In his mid-thirties, Mariano was short, rotund, and beleaguered — a disciple of Josimo's working in a hostile parish, but stout-hearted and determined to be true to his call. He drove a large Chevy pickup, a rancher's car, which was somehow incongruous, and took herbal tea for his triglycerides.

"I came to the seminary here in Tocantinópolis in 1975," he told me. "Josimo was going to São Paulo to do Philosophy and Literature and he dropped me off here. He and I became great friends and every vacation we got to know each other better, although I was at the beginning of my studies and he was far advanced. There was a lot of difference between our levels of intelligence and courage, but we got on well. I always thought of him as a master. I wanted to be like him.

"He was ordained in 1979. The year before that, I was invited by the Italian padre of Wanderlândia to go and live there. So I had the privilege of working with Josimo, and we got to know each other well. Then Padre Atílio left, and Josimo took over the parish. I lived with him and Dona Olinda. Josimo was her only son, and she loved to spoil him. She treated me like a son too.

" I learned a lot in theyear and a half that I lived with him. In all that time, I never saw him angry or upset; he was always smiling. He was really smart. Cultured, yet simple. He always had the right word, a little joke, he was never cross, and he never lost his cool, even when he was dealing with violent people who wanted to kill him.

"There was a lot of conflict in the area at that time. As Josimo got to be better known, he began to take on the job of protecting the peasants and telling them about their rights. Of course, he aroused a lot of hatred on the part of the ranchers.

"He used to look just like a peasant, you know! When he was at seminary, I remember he looked like a boy from the backwoods — rumpled old clothes, pants rolled up, a real hick. He used to wear those boots they use for working in the fields. The bishop thought they were ugly, and wanted to buy him some shoes, but he said he didn't want any. Dom Cornélio used to kid him and say he should be obedient, but he wore those boots until they fell apart! He told me that story one day when we were having a beer together.

"Another argument he had with the bishop was about his mustache. Dom Cornélio wanted him to shave it off because the other priests — most of them were Italians at that time — were clean shaven. Josimo said, 'Look, I don't think a mustache will alter anything in me. It won't add anything or take anything away, so I won't take it off.' Dom Cornélio said 'If you want to obey the bishop, you'll take off your mustache.' But he wouldn't. He wanted to be a priest with a mustache. Dom Cornélio didn't really mind; he loved him like a son.

"Later on, the other bishop, Dom Aloísio, asked Josimo to leave Wanderlândia and take over the Pastoral Land Commission.

Josimo had previously worked with them, but not in an official capacity. So he took on the job of diocesan coordinator, and he moved to São Sebastião in the Parrot's Beak. He got right down to work. In a sense it was his chance to form the church of his dreams. But he never got to see the fruits of his labor.

"Josimo was an unforgettable person. Immortal, really. He's very alive in this diocese, which he didn't used to be. At the time, it was only the people in the Parrot's Beak who loved him, and not all of them either. But now at last he's known and loved by many more people. The majority of his fellow priests never understood his work, you see. There was a lot of hostility, particularly from the older ones. They didn't understand him and they didn't understand his work in the CPT, although they respected him and understood his capabilities. He was persecuted and despised, although he never took it all that seriously when people disagreed with him. Even when they attacked his ideas and his work, he never let it get him down, and he never stopped the dialogue.

"People used to call him radical, extremist, but he wasn't that way at all. He was extremely open. He would talk to anyone. I know people who are doing the same work as he did, and they won't even sit at the same table as the opposition, but that was never Josimo's way. He was open to anything.

"The thing is that the people in São Sebastião didn't appreciate him when he was there. Most of his parishioners didn't like him. He had more friends in Buriti, but he had a lot of enemies there too. He always had to have men guarding the door of the church when he was saying Mass. I think he must have been very lonely and isolated. He asked me to stay on with him, but unfortunately I could only live eighteen months with him. To me, he was a master. He taught me that if we work in the church of the poor, we have to opt for the poor, heart and soul.

"That didn't mean he didn't enjoy life. I remember him coming to the seminary and playing football with us. He was a good player. He was good at lots of things. He danced the samba well, he sang well, he prayed well, he wrote well. He was very jokey, very extroverted. You couldn't help liking him. Afterwards they used to describe him as a dangerous and violent man, but that was all wrong. Strong, yes. He was a man with a strong sense of mission, and he never wavered. But violent — never.

"It was an extraordinary that someone of his age could die. He died at the same age I was when I was ordained. And for what? For love... He was very courageous. He was never a coward, he never ran away. And he was never a sensationalist, never did anything to draw attention to himself. He was simple. He could speak with intellectuals and peasants with the same unaffectedness. I once spent a week with him, and we went round the villages. I remember him preaching at Mass and talking of people in terms of fruits and flowers: *cupuaçu*, oranges and bananas. He wanted to explain that we're all important. We're all special, but we don't all have to be the same. He spoke the language of the people, and they loved him for it.

"I'll never forget him. Wherever I go, I'll always remember him, my friend and companion, a man who loved his priesthood and gave himself for the love of God. Josimo never wanted the glory for himself. He was a man who was internationally known before his death, but he never wanted to be famous.

"To me he's still alive. He does miracles, even in Tocantinópolis where he was most neglected. He was hated here by the ranchers and by most people, come to that. They didn't agree with his work and they rejected him. I want them to see him as he was: a man, a priest, someone who freely laid down his life. Like it says in the Gospel, there is no greater love...

"I'll tell you something. I myself have never taken the same stand as Josimo. I've never made his explicit option for the poor. But the day I do, they'll crucify me, too."

Chapter Four

This Land is My Land

A fertile land well watered by the rivers Araguaia and Tocantins, the Parrot's Beak provided a haven for the early settlers. Dona Raimunda sang us a song about it when we were together at Mata Seca:

Before they built Brasília
this was a place
of perfect silence
and no problems at all.
It was a real paradise
which provided us with all our needs,
all we had to do was work the land.

The first comers
cut their patch of forest
opened up a clearing
with their hands, their hoes, their machetes.
And then others started to arrive
and put in their fields,
and so the population grew.

It was a region
where people lived in peace,
poor but happy,
working their fields
without trying to get ahead of one another
welcoming newcomers
and building up their villages.
And then those families
who settled here
thatched their houses
with babassu leaves,
moved into their houses
lived on their lands,
hunted and fished.

Each year they put their fields
wherever they wanted.

There was land to spare,
that's why they came here,
opening up the forest
without fear of the mighty
who they'd never seen.

And so all these settlers
lived here in peace,
they held the land in common,
nobody had fences or boundaries.
They never thought that the land-grabbers
would come and throw them off
their sacred lands.

While the settlers were living out their Wordsworthian idyll in the Parrot's Beak, far away in Brasília, government planners were marking their maps with bold strokes representing the great new highways: Belem-Brasília and the Transamazônica. The Parrot's Beak was located near the intersection between the two, and as the bulldozers and construction gangs forged their way through the forest, they brought with them the end of an era. Migrants poured up the Belem-Brasília highway from the south and some of the more intrepid headed west along the Transamazônica.

Some of the migrants were landless peasants from the dry lands in the northeast, but others were adventurers — businessmen, industrialists, large landowners from the south — lured by the myth of the frontier, and the prospect of acquiring huge areas of land at little or no cost, land that might, with luck, increase its value two, five, ten, a hundredfold.

Land-grabbing is an ancient art in Brazil, and its practitioners have developed a large repertoire of tricks. Their aim is to obtain title by whatever means necessary, an effort made considerably easier by the fact that no one has a very clear notion of the land titling situation anyway. The first division of the New World was made by the Pope in 1494 at the Treaty of Tordesilhas, when he drew a line on the map of South America, granting all the land to the west to Spain, and all the land to the east to Portugal. In colonial times, the Portuguese crown had rewarded its favorites with enormous tracts of land in much the same way as colonial powers had handed out large areas in the United States. In settled areas along the river banks, some titles were issued by the state, others by the parish. Extractive rights were sometimes granted, and those who worked unclaimed lands for a year and a day were eligible to acquire squatters' rights — in those rare cases where they had heard of such a thing or were in a position to enforce their claims. The huge sparsely inhabited lands of the interior were claimed by the federal government, which in 1964 also claimed all land lying along federal highways — to a depth of from six to sixty miles.

Amid such a riot of conflicting titling, the way was open to any and every unscrupulous person who wished to make himself rich. Local judges, doctors, architects, businessmen and city officials fell over one another to hire the services of those expert in falsifying documents. It was pitifully easy. Blank title deeds could be picked up from land registry offices and filled in to suit. At the stroke of a pen, holdings could be increased and survey maps could be redesigned. Documents could be artificially aged to prove prior claim.

The newcomers might even buy the squatters out, offering them laughably low prices. Since the squatters had no clear notion of the cash value of their lands, they often let them go for next to nothing. If they seemed unwilling to negotiate, they would receive a visit from a hired gunman, and if they didn't take him seriously, they could expect all sorts of unpleasant consequences — beatings, theft, intimidation, even arson. Not that such strong-arm methods were always required. The new "landowner" could always invoke the power of the law, and serve eviction orders on the often illiterate peasants. These would be delivered by heavily armed police, often accompanied by the land-grabber's "employees" (gunmen). In order to discourage the peasants from returning, it was not uncommon for police to take part in burning down the squatters' houses, destroying their crops and beating them up. Terrified and destitute, they had no choice then but to flee for their lives.

Needless to say, not all of the ranchers were villains, nor were all the squatters saints. But from the start, the odds were stacked heavily in favor of the former. For one thing, the whole area had recently been under military control. In the early '70s, there had been some skirmishes between the army and a small band of urban guerrillas settled in the forest across the Araguaia river in southern Pará. Although the guerrillas never numbered more than a hundred, they caused enough disruption to tie up a force of twenty thousand soldiers for more than two years. The presence of such unexpected resistance on the fringes of civilization made the federal government determined to tame the area, and they invoked the National Security Laws. A special task force was created to monitor the land situation in the region. It was christened GETAT, the Executive Group for the Lands of the Araguaia/Tocantins Region. One of the legendary figures of the day was Major Curió, a character straight out of a cowboy movie who was fond of making dramatic appearances, firing from the hip and announcing that he was the fastest gun in the Amazon. Major Curió was nicknamed after a songbird, on account of his habit of roughing up his prisoners until they "sang." The government put him in charge of a group of unruly gold miners in Serra Pelada who loved him and referred to him as Papa Curió. But the inhabitants of the Parrot's Beak disliked and feared him, particularly after he started bombing them...

Caught between the iron grip of the military, the police, and the politically powerful landowners, most of the settlers had no option but to get out. João Custódio, the union leader whom I had met at Mata Seca, was one of those who resisted.

I went to visit João Custódio in Sumauma, a small, primitive village with a sandy road running through the middle. A recent mayor has built a nice new communal wash house, which remains unused because there is no water supply to it, although they have tried to sink a well on three different sites. The drilling equipment is stacked untidily by the side of the road, beginning to rust. There is a health post, but it's locked. No medicine, no nurse. But there is electricity, and João's house was one of the few houses that was connected. The union operated by the light of small rustic oil lamps. The priest, a foreigner, recently constructed an impressive church. The money for the building came from Italy.

The local bus rattled along the main street, upsetting the tranquil grazing of donkeys, pigs and white cattle. It groaned to a halt in the middle of the village. João Custódio was waiting for me on a bench outside his front door. His house was made of wattle and daub, and as we entered, my first impression was that the house was totally empty. We stepped down into a large room furnished only with a rickety table on which reposed a water filter. There was a picture of Josimo on the wall. The room next door held a smaller table and chairs, and a low partition wall separated an empty space destined to be the new kitchen. One of the bedrooms had a large bed covered with a patchwork quilt — the only bed in the house. Everyone else slept in hammocks. The kitchen in the back was nothing but a small mud stove and a couple of aluminum pots. In the yard, there was a well, a small wooden platform surrounded by walls of woven palm which served as the bathroom, and a privy with a concrete base. Joâo's wife, Maria, was as much of an activist as he was. There was one child in evidence, a good looking boy of eight. Two sons were at the gold mines, one of their daughters had become a prostitute. and the other had been sent to live with Josimo's mother, Dona Olinda, whom they hoped would keep her out of trouble and send her to school. But she was a wild little thing, who ran off into the bush to smoke tobacco. Maria had been criticized by other women for giving her child away. Her remaining son, the youngest, was the joy of her heart.

Joâo and I took a couple of stools under a tree behind the house, and talked in the late afternoon.

"I got here in '79," he began. "Things were already very bad. There were police and *pistoleiros* all over the place, and people were losing their land on all sides. We didn't know what to do about it. The padres didn't do anything for us, there weren't any unions, and we'd never heard of the Pastoral Land Commission.

"I remember the day I was arrested. It was July 20th, 1980. The police picked up a whole bunch of us out in the fields. They locked us up in the house of a rancher called Zé Ferreira, and we couldn't see how we were ever going to get out. In the end, the police let us go, giving us two weeks to clear off the land, and never return. Imagine that! It was our land; it didn't belong to Zé Ferreira. Some of us had been here thirty years before he arrived. He said we'd invaded his land, but it was just the opposite. He was the invader! Of course we weren't going to leave.

"Just after that, a group showed up from the Pastoral Land Commission. We had no idea who they were. We'd never heard of them. In fact, we thought they were something to do with Zé Ferreira. Naturally, none of us wanted to talk to them. But after a while, I got curious, so I went over to see what was going on. One of the group was a foreigner — I couldn't understand what he was saying. I said to him, 'Can't you speak Brazilian?' He laughed and pointed to the woman with him. I could understand her all right.

We got to talking about the land situation, and she asked us if there was anyone in the community who could help us in our struggle. I said, 'Only God.'

"By that stage, we'd collected forty armed men and were all set to fight it out with Zé Ferreira, but the CPT people told us we should fight through the courts instead. They said that violence wouldn't help, since it only leads to more violence. They said they'd help us out and they did.

"In 1981, we had a demonstration in Imperatriz against GETAT, the government agency in charge of the lands in the Araguaia/Tocantins region. They were supposed to be sorting out the titling, but as far as we could see they never did a thing on our behalf. We had a demonstration and demanded our land. The head of GETAT, Colonel Lisboa, promised us that he would settle the matter in 15 days. And so he did. He came with the police and twelve *pistoleiros,* and got the ranchers to loose their cattle in our fields. They stole all our rice too. One man lost 120 sacks of rice; four other people lost everything they had harvested.

"Things went from bad to worse. Zé Ferreira — the rancher I mentioned before — caught one of the squatters, stuck a pistol in his mouth, beat him up and sent him to tell us that he was ready for a fight. So there was nothing for it. We had a big shoot-out, we overturned his Toyota and he took to his heels. It was only by the grace of God that no one died

"Josimo came on the scene in '83. The first time he appeared, we didn't know he was a priest. He told us he was born in Pará, lived in Xambioá, was a teacher and had just moved to the parish of São Sebastião. He told us he was working in the CPT, and he told us about the Workers' Party (that's the PT) and the unions. He told us not to slug it out with the ranchers. He said it was better to take them to court. He said he'd go with us to Brasília to make sure we got our rights, and he did.

"He taught us a bit of the Gospel as well. He used to tell us that people were all equal: blacks, whites, Indians, everybody. Personally, I wouldn't have thought that was a sin, but I think the authorities thought so.

"They started talking about land reform around that time. A group of leaders gathered together to discuss how we were going to get it going. We needed documents. I said I'd do the work in Sítio

Novo. I worked right under the nose of the ranchers with the *pistoleiros* waving their guns about. We had a demonstration in Augustinópolis, and in 1985 we went in a bus to Brasília to see Paulo Brossard, the Justice Minister. The Council of Bishops supported us too.

"And it worked out in the end, because the authorities came in and divided the land into forty-eight lots. But they never gave us title. We don't have title to this day."

1979 was also the year that another well-known figure arrived in the area. Dona Cota lives in Esperantina, the very last village at the tip of the Parrot's Beak. A striking-looking woman with bright blue eyes, she gets around at a great rate despite a club foot. Small and feisty, she is a bonny fighter or a damn nuisance, depending on which side you support.

"My family came here from Augustinópolis in 1979," she told me. "No one was living here at the time except Pedro Sousa. It was thick forest. We came along with three other families, made our clearings in the forest and collected babassu nuts. One day, someone denounced Pedro Sousa to the police, saying he was a *pistoleiro* who had two hundred armed men hiding in the forest. It was all because he wanted to get his hands on our land. I never heard such nonsense. Then Major Curió went to Pedro's house with a whole lot of police and they started shooting. Everyone ran away and hid in the forest.

"A few days later the police came back and told us we must give Pedro up. So we went to find him. He didn't want to come out, but we told him he must. That time it was only a couple of policemen and Major Curió, who said he just wanted to have a little chat with Pedro, and promised no harm would come to him. Major Curió offered him a ride in his helicopter, and Pedro went off all smiles. But they beat him up, and then do you know what they did? They dropped a bomb on the village of Sampaio and scared everyone to death."

Natividade was living in Sampaio when they dropped the bomb. On the day I went to meet her, the bus had broken down, so I shared the back of a hot dusty pick-up with four teenage boys and the local schoolteacher. Half choked by exhaust fumes, I reeled out onto the sandy street of Sampaio and set off to find Natividade.

The primitive wattle and daub houses crouched next to each other, their low shaggy thatch roofs looking as if they could do with a trim. Natividade, a nut-brown woman, was sitting on a rawhide stool outside her house.

"You want to know about Major Curió?" she grinned at me. "Nastiest character you could hope to meet. On that famous day, I was on the other side of the river planting beans with my brother, when I heard this helicopter. Suddenly there was a terrific explosion and smoke all over. I thought: Shit! They've flattened the whole place. We crossed the river in ten minutes flat, and when we got here we said: My God, they've dropped a bomb on the beach. We saw this huge hole.

"It was Major Curió. Called us all to a meeting, he did. I was so furious about it, I said to my brother: whatever happens, I'm not going. But my brother went and told me about it afterwards. Major Curió said that this time they'd dropped a bomb, but next time they'd kill us because we were terrorists. Someone had told them we had four hundred armed men here. Afterwards, we heard they'd picked up Nicola, the missionary, on the accusation of his being a communist subversive, or some such lie. They hung him out of the helicopter and pretended they were going to shoot him. I'm surprised the poor man didn't die of fright."

Chapter Five

Building the Church of the Poor

Josimo didn't get a very warm welcome when he moved to São Sebastião. The previous incumbent had been an old-style priest from Poland named Stanislau, who believed that a priest's job was to stay in his church and say Mass. He'd listen to confessions, he'd go to the ranches for weddings and christenings, but he wouldn't dream of getting mixed up in politics. He had a horror of anything that smacked of communism and was later moved to criticize his successor in a most unchristian fashion.

Josimo's idea of the priesthood was completely different, and most of the people in São Sebastião didn't think much of it. Having a black priest was bad enough, but this one didn't even say Mass every Sunday. Josimo was always getting into that ancient car of his and rushing off round the villages, and he spent altogether too much time talking about the land. He held inflammatory notions about human rights. It wasn't the job of the church to get mixed up in that sort of thing, and they told him so repeatedly.

Then there was the ridiculous fuss he made about baptisms. He refused to do them without giving preparation classes. As a result, Josimo's parishioners used to defect en masse to Augustinópolis where the priest was more accommodating. Josimo wouldn't go out to barbecues and weddings on the ranches, but he'd trail all over the bush to the smallest communities. It was a clear case of wrong priorities.

They couldn't figure it out. Why would he be so interested in the land, anyway? It wasn't as if he had any. He used to laugh and say the only land he had was the dirt under his fingernails. It was true: he did look a mess, always going around in flip-flops and old shirts. He didn't even look like a proper priest.

Then there was the question of the union. Josimo was always going on about unions and politics — a lot of socialist nonsense. Like as not, he was a communist too. A black man and a communist who didn't even say Mass every Sunday!

Zé Carneiro, the mayor, didn't like Josimo. He didn't like him when he arrived and he detested him heartily by the time he died. People said the mayor was one of those involved in Josimo's death, and that his deputy was just as bad. The mayor was a vain man whose style of governing ran very much to the bread and circuses model, although he was a cultured man in his way and generally spoke politely. He became bitterly jealous of Josimo. They were always coming up against each other, in public at least. When he had the row with Josimo over the telephone exchange, he was heard to say that he'd show Josimo who was boss in his town. He told Josimo to keep his hands off the school because he was turning all the staff against him. He finally ordered the teachers to stay away from the church if they wanted to keep their jobs. Later he was heard to remark that that black priest would have to be gotten rid of, by whatever means.

One might expect the mayor and the landowners to dislike Josimo; it was perhaps more surprising that many of his poorer parishioners did, also. They, too, were accustomed to the old-style paternalist priest, and they were used to going along with the opinions of the authorities. So naturally they sided against those few who did support Josimo. The Mothers' Union reckoned that the parish hall belonged to them, and once they mounted an attack on a small group that was doing a Bible study there. Waving their brooms and kitchen knives, they advanced on the room, egged on by their menfolk in the background. When the Bible study group burst into song, the aggressors backed off.

Sergeant Mendes, the sheriff, and his sidekick, Nego Chaves, found Josimo a damn nuisance. He was always interfering in matters that didn't concern him, and worse still, denouncing the police for violence.

But after their initial surprise, some of the people — mostly those who had never taken part in church activities before — found themselves drawn in. Previously they had stood outside the church door; now Josimo persuaded them to come inside. "He was so cheerful," one of them told me. "He loved to sing and play the guitar. He was always playing with the kids, chatting to everyone. He never left anyone out. Before he came, I used to think I couldn't do anything. But he gave me confidence. I never thought I'd be able to talk to a priest like that, but he was just like family. I'm not very smart, but he was smart enough for all of us."

"He was a man of deep faith," said one of the men. "His God was the God who walks with us day by day. He used to pray from our lives, not from books. He was never afraid. I remember once spending the night with him in the forest, because there was a *pistoleiro* after us."

"We were like a plant dying for lack of water," said a woman. "And he came and watered it. He taught us how to look after it. And now it's grown into a tree and it's bearing fruit."

"He made us believe in ourselves," said one girl, a little hesitantly. "He showed us that the poor are God's instruments who will build a new heaven and a new earth."

For Josimo, there was so much to do, so little time. So much love to give, and who would love him back? His first task was to build up the church. The people had been used to sitting passively through Mass, and Josimo sensed they didn't really know what it was to be followers of Christ. He wanted them to understand that "church" wasn't a spectator sport, but a way of living and forging community. He wanted them to open their Bibles and come face to face with Christ. He wanted them to take responsibility for their lives, and not to be victimized any longer. He wanted them to understand that they could change things, even the terrible things happening around them. He wanted them to live and work together, to be accountable to each other, to defend and encourage each other, to become strong together.

In search of Josimo, I visited the parish house in São Sebastião. A large gaunt building, it backs onto the church. These days, the parish is run by a couple of Jesuit priests and a seminarian. Padre Miguel, a stout figure with a tangled grey beard, was bent over the greasy engine of the parish Toyota. Cars need a lot of maintenance on Amazonian roads, there is always something that is falling off and needs to be fixed. Miguel disentangled himself from the bowels of the Toyota, gave me a disturbingly shrewd look, wiped his oily hands on his sagging shorts, and led me into the office.

"To understand the sort of problems Josimo faced, you need to know a bit about the background here," he told me. "People here are not united. They can't see that if they work together they can make a decent living. We need to change that.

"Until recently, they lived in a subsistence economy. There was always game in the forest, fish in the rivers; they planted a bit of rice, a bit of manioc and they did fine. They didn't need much. If they got sick, they used plants from the forest. They lived off the land and they were content.

"Then suddenly, everything changed. There was no forest left, nothing to hunt. They had to buy meat and medicine. They had to send their kids to school, had to buy clothes and books for them. Instead of using wood, they had to pay for electricity and gas. They needed money. The land used to provide them with a living and then it didn't any more. They found they needed things. They had to change. Capitalism had arrived. When they were in the forest, they didn't have to store things. There wasn't any point. If the rice harvest was good and there was anything over, they couldn't sell it because there were no roads. So they lost it. They operated on a very short time scale. They didn't plan ahead. But now they have to start thinking about the future. In those days, if they got sick they either got better or they died. Now they have to pay the taxi to take them to hospital, they have to buy medicines, they have to plan a little. So they prefer to go to work in such industries as we have, say a sawmill. They don't earn a lot but they get it every week. It's cash in hand. If they work on the land, they don't have ready money all the time. What we need to prove to them is that the land can provide food, subsistence, somewhere to live and something to live on. But they're going to have to change their methods and plant different things — fruit trees, coffee, bananas. I think the big problem is changing their thinking patterns.

"One of the interesting things that Josimo did was work with women's groups. Women are more open to change than men. They're the ones that have to put the food on the table for the family. Often it's the women who keep the family going by making babassu oil. The husband goes off to the goldmines, and the wife stays and does whatever she can to keep her children alive. She understands the need to get together with others. The women have set up associations in four of the communities, and they've started a day care center in Buriti. They work with the nuns on child care, learning about health and nutrition. Josimo realized the importance of working with the women. Women are smart.

"I think he got more support from the women than the men. That's often the case, you know. But Josimo's trouble was the prejudice against him. The parish priest usually commands a lot of respect, particularly in rural areas like these. But there were people here who simply couldn't accept a black priest. They were dreadful to him. They used to make fun of him and call him 'that black monkey.' And of course they called him a communist — not that they had any idea what a communist was. They got the word from the ranchers, a hangover from the days of the guerrillas. The army used to scare people by talking about communists as if they were some kind of monster. There was a lot of talk about guerrillas, assassins, communists, terrorists. The *pistoleiro* who killed Josimo said he killed a communist. He didn't know what a communist was. Just like a child, he didn't know what it is, only that he doesn't like it.

"All this is important because you might be tempted to think of Josimo as if he were some Christ-like figure, some martyr who was mourned by everyone. What you need to understand is that most people hated his guts."

Somewhat sobered by this verdict from the Jesuit priest, I went to talk to the crew which was cleaning out the church in preparation for that night's Mass. Instead of the usual old crones with their heads wrapped in black scarves, I was surprised to find two young women in jeans and the seminarian, on his hands and knees, sorting out the wiring.

"We never used to go inside the church before," one of the women told me, dropping her broom, and settling down on the step. "We used to stand at the church door and watch the Mass as if we were watching television. That was it. We never got to talk to the padre. When Josimo came, the ranchers boycotted the church. So did most of the townspeople. There was hardly anyone left. A few of us started hanging round the church door, out of curiosity as much as anything else. And Josimo invited us in. He said he couldn't run the church by himself, and he needed our help. I never expected to get dragged in like that, I just thought I'd help out for a few day until someone else came along. I did it because I was sorry for him, and I thought people had treated him badly. I never realized how much fun it would be. I never thought it would be a whole new beginning.

"He taught us about the Bible. He used to involve us in the services by asking us to read or to sing, and then he'd help us understand what we were doing. He had a wonderful way with people, he used to persuade everyone to join in. We'd always thought we couldn't do it, you see, because we couldn't read. But he'd say, 'That's nonsense! You may not be able to read much but you were born smart.' He taught us to read the Bible, and then he used to ask us what we thought. He used to get everyone to give their opinion, and he never told us we'd got it wrong. He'd say, 'That's it! You've got it right.'

"He made us understand what it was to be a Christian. He said a Christian was someone who was a follower of Jesus Christ. He was a good organizer, too. When we had our saints' day festivals, he used to go and visit each street and he'd say, 'OK, you have to decide who's going to prepare the Mass, who's going to do the food, who'll do the raffle.' I remember once I made a cake for the festival. It was a disaster! I was so ashamed, and I couldn't make another because I didn't have the ingredients. Josimo came and took some crumbs off the top and he said, 'Oh, Marlene, it's delicious!' He told me it's no good taking a wonderful cake up to the altar to show how clever we are. What counts with God is our good will.

"You should go and see the nuns, really." Marlene brushed her hair out of her eyes and picked up her broom in a determined fashion. "Go talk to them. They knew Josimo as well as anybody."

The day I went to the Centro dos Mulatos to find the nuns, it had been raining so hard that even the JAMJOY bus couldn't make it. I took a ride in a cattle truck instead. Mulatos is a miserable little place, and the Sisters live, like everyone else, in a mud house with a shaggy thatch roof. The white ants have got into the roof timbers and they need replacing; meanwhile the roof is inadequately covered in black plastic. Stepping over the gate — "Keeps the pigs out," Sister Bia explained bluntly — I found myself in a simple room with a beaten earth floor, a large table surrounded by rawhide stools, a counter, a gas stove, and some shelves stacked with crockery and cutlery. Over the stove they had tacked up a poster of the National Council of Women Rural Workers, and on the wooden door, someone had sketched the face of Christ.

Sister Mada is tall and fair. She looks German. Sister Bia is shorter and wiry. Both in their fifties, they are dressed in jeans and tee shirts. "We used to wear habits," Mada told me. "But we decided jeans were more practical. And we dropped the 'Sister' bit. We found it put people off."

"We hoped you'd be here for lunch," grinned Bia. "We love having guests. It gives us an excuse to have dessert."

We sat round the table drinking soup and the nuns told me something of their early days in the Bico.

"We got here in 1980," Bia said. "We'd come from Mato Grosso, so we were used to living at the back of beyond. It was our bishop, Dom Pedro Casaldaliga, who suggested we come to the Parrot's Beak. He said there'd be plenty for us to do! Josimo was the curate in Wanderlândia when we first came to take a look round. We stayed with him and traveled all round the diocese. We thought of staying in his parish, but in the end we decided this was the place for us. The local padre used to spend almost all his time in São Sebastião, so it was up to us to organize the church work in the villages. Our ideas about church were just about the opposite of his, but we tried not to annoy him too much. We didn't see a lot of him in any case, because we were always tearing round the villages on our bikes. It wasn't until later that we got a car.

"There was another couple of nuns living in Sampaio, Lurdinha and Nicole, and we were all on the same wavelength. When Josimo came to São Sebastião, it was like a breath of fresh air. We were able to plan things much better, and things were more fairly distributed. Josimo used to say that all the communities had the same needs and the same rights, and they should have a Mass at least once a month. We divided the parish into four districts.

"Josimo used to have a very heavy program at weekends because he was always in one of the four districts. He used to give Bible studies and have several Masses a day. He used to come here the first weekend of every month, and he'd cover Esperantina and the neighboring communities. Of course, the people in São Sebastião didn't like that because they'd been used to having Mass every Sunday. Josimo never had many friends in São Sebastião, partly for that reason. Another reason was that most of the people there used to work in the town hall. They were under the thumb of the mayor

He used to give them little presents to keep them sweet. The people in São Sebastião didn't work on the land like they did in Buriti, and here in Mulatos and in Esperantina.

"Josimo did most of his work for the CPT in this area. There were lots of extremely serious land conflicts, and he was always ready to support the people, tell them about their rights, bring in lawyers, denounce miscarriages of justice and that sort of thing. When people were chucked out, he'd be there with them, and first thing he'd do would be help them organize so that they could go back in. 'It's your land,' he used to say, 'and you must defend it because it's all you've got.' He'd always encourage them to work together, form a community association, join the rural workers' union. He kept telling them they'd be stronger if they stuck together. He encouraged them to learn about politics and to participate. They'd spent twenty years under a military dictatorship, and they didn't understand what it was to be free people. He was a member of the Workers' Party: the PT. People were always getting muddled between the PT and the CPT, and we used to explain that the PT was a political party and the CPT was church work, but they got confused anyway. Still do!

"Sister Lurdinha was a keen member of the PT, so keen that she finally left the church and ran for the local council on the PT ticket. She was always completely fearless and she couldn't stand to see injustice. She and Josimo used to tell the press what was happening, they used to contact the state government, and sometimes they even went to Brasília.

"They really made a lot of enemies that way — the ranchers, the politicians, the police, many of the workers, and even the other priests who didn't understand what they were trying to do. I think the day that Josimo became the CPT diocesan coordinator was the day he signed his death warrant. But we didn't see it at the time. The first time we really ran into trouble was the day we had the demonstration for Land Reform in Augustinópolis. It was the first time the landless had publicly stood up for their rights, and of course the landowners didn't like it at all!"

♦ **Chapter Six** ♦

Blood and Fire

Once upon a time in the Parrot's Beak, there was a flourishing settlement called the Centro dos Canários. Women sat together chatting while they cracked the babassu nuts for oil, men went off to the fields and planted rice and beans, corn and manioc, children gathered firewood and played in the dust. There were thirty-three houses in the settlement, and a total of two hundred and forty people living there. They lived well. The last rice harvest had yielded sixteen hundred bags, the best year since the first arrivals had made their clearing in the forest seventeen years earlier. The people of Canários were content as they started to plan for the rainy season planting.

All of a sudden, the villagers had a nasty surprise. On a hot afternoon at the end of May, 1984, a dusty jeep wheezed up the track to the village and out stepped an unknown man carrying a large envelope. One of the children ran up to see who it was. "Take me to your father," he commanded. "He's out in the fields," stammered the child. "Your mother, then," he said, and the child skipped into the nearest house.

A woman came out, smoothing her hair. "I've brought you a court order," said the man. "It says that this land has been bought by José Marcelino de Queiroz, better known as Palmério, and that from now on you are going to have to pay him rent."

"Whatever do you mean?" said the woman stoutly. "We've never heard of this man Palmério, and what's more, this land is ours and we're not paying rent to anyone."

"Just doing my job, " said the man, and climbed back into his car.

There was much anxious discussion in the village that night, but on one point everyone was agreed: the land belonged to them. "It's our land," they reassured one another. "They can't do anything to us."

The days and weeks went past, and nothing happened. On the last day of July, the jeep returned. This time, the men were at home and one of them stepped forward to talk to the driver. "I have a document here," said the driver, "which says that the following people are to appear at court in Itaguatins on August 10th." He read out a long list of names, none of them correctly written. "It's to do with the rent you owe Palmério," he explained.

The men looked at one another in consternation. "I'll go," said one of the braver ones. "There must be some mistake. I'll go and sort it out."

"I'll come with you," said one of his friends valiantly.

So they went. It was more than sixty miles away, and the journey took them three days. It would have taken longer if they hadn't gotten a ride on a truck for part of the way. They couldn't make head or tail of the hearing, but they did their best to explain that the land was theirs and that they'd never heard of anyone called Palmério. "How can he possibly say it's his land if he's never been anywhere near it?" they asked anxiously. But the judge didn't seem to understand. "Palmério owns the title to the land and you're going to have to pay up and that's that," he announced. The two men set off on their journey home, bearing the news.

The villagers spent a long time discussing the matter, but they couldn't come to any conclusions, and in any case there was no time to waste, what with the rainy season just round the corner and the land to be prepared.

September 25th, 1984, was a hot humid day. The men were returning from the fields for their morning meal when a truck appeared carrying ten armed policemen and a man from the court in Itaguatins. "Right, folks," he announced. "This is it. I have an order to evict the whole village."

The villagers stared at him in stunned silence.

"Everyone out of the houses," snapped the police sergeant. "Get in there and find their guns," he gestured to his men. "Right, you and you and you," he pointed at the three nearest men. "And you two," selecting two more. "Down on your knees, you sons of bitches." The men hesitated and he pointed his gun in their direction. The women stood silently as the policemen ransacked their houses, tore open mattresses, emptied out the sacks of rice, pounced on hunting rifles, machetes and even kitchen knives, and seized such money as they could find. One young man tried to restrain the police, and was savagely beaten and kicked for his pains.

Some of the children ran off into the forest to hide, and a pregnant woman fainted. The rest of the village stood there in smoldering silence.

"Now listen here," the sergeant turned to the huddled men. "You've got ten days to get out, bag and baggage, and don't forget the pigs and chickens. Me and my men are coming back here next week and we're going to set fire to every house in the place, with everything and everyone inside them."

There's no arguing with brute force. Slowly and numbly the villagers packed up their possessions and left. Nine days later, the village was burnt to the ground.

Among the sad little band of the dispossessed was a young couple called Manoel and Maria. Maria was heavily pregnant. Together with her husband and small child, she fled the village and took refuge in a tumble-down shack. It was here that her child was born, and she called him Raimundo — the light of the world.

Josimo wrote a poem about it.

> Great suffering,
> torture, humiliation,
> beatings and arrests
> have invaded the dwellings of the poor.
> Manoel, a laborer,
> husband of Maria Raimunda,
> was desperate, with no place to go.
> Maria Raimunda, pregnant,
> did not know where to turn.
> Maria and Manoel,
> driven out at gunpoint,
> walked in loneliness.
> Night fell,
> a barn provided shelter for Manoel,
> Maria, and a year old child.
> Maria swept and cleaned out
> the cow dung.
>
> The day they burned the village
> was a day of terror.

The enemies of life said
'Where is your God?
Why doesn't he come to help you?
Where are the Fathers and the Sisters,
your defenders?'

Maria Raimunda gave birth to a child
in the bleak stable.
And all the poor,
fleeing the tribulation,
came to greet the child.
They called him Raimundo,
because a ray of life recreated the world.

Amidst the struggle,
in the heat of battle,
amidst the domination of the powerful,
a child was born,
a symbol of hope.

Laurenço Almeida Lima, father of nine, had been living in Canários for nine years.

"I remember I was in Axixá when I heard that the police had gone into Canários," he wrote. "So I went along to see what was going on. I found my wife hiding in the forest and she begged me not to go, but I felt I had to. I'd no sooner got to my house than three policemen burst in, and started hitting me. They asked for my gun and I said I didn't have one. I looked outside and saw the five men kneeling in the sun. The police asked me which of them owned a gun, and I told them we were laborers, not bandits. Then the sergeant said to us, 'Well, you're going to have to move out of here. You've all disobeyed the order of the judge. The truck will come and take you to the road: rice, dogs, pigs, goats, and all. Then you're on your own. You can take everything but you can't stay and work in the fields. You can take your whole house if you want.'

"After that the police grabbed me again, marched me off into the forest, and started roughing me up and asking about guns. They hit me over the head with a revolver butt. Pushed my face down into the mud. I thought I was going to drown. They dunked me four times. Then one of them drew his revolver, and I could see from his expression that he was going to shoot me. I just lay there waiting to die. Then, for some reason, the sergeant told him not to kill me. 'We'll give him a good hiding,' he said. I said to them, 'Just go ahead and kill me while you're at it,' and the sergeant laughed and said to me, 'Not so fast, you son of a bitch. First, you're going to wash that ugly mug of yours in the mud.' Then they hauled me to my feet and told me to walk ahead. I was sure they were going to shoot me, but they kept kicking me and hitting me and insisting I tell them the names of those who had guns. I kept stumbling and falling and finally they got tired of persecuting me and went off to find someone else.

"I crawled off into the forest. I remember I was aching all over and I could hear gunshots in the village. I found my wife again; she was still in the same place where I had left her. We decided to make for Juverlândia. I had lost my shoes in the scuffle and I had to walk without them. It took us four hours to get there."

Laurenço's daughter, Maria, was in the village of Axixá at the time. She heard that there had been trouble in Canários and that her father had been beaten up. "I went to look for my father but I didn't know where he had gone," she wrote. "He didn't get here till after ten at night. I was so angry when I saw him that I went down to the police station to register a complaint. While I was there, rancher Palmério arrived with four policemen in his jeep. They said hello but I didn't answer. Then another bunch of policemen arrived; one of them was short and fat and only had one eye. I heard the lieutenant saying, 'You can't be soft on these bandits because if you turn your back, they'll fire at you.' I waited for the sheriff and told him I wanted to register a complaint. He told me I couldn't because the whole thing was perfectly legal. He said they had a judge's order and everything."

Joâo Filho was also there that day. Black, strong, he has a wonderful smile, even though it's short on teeth.

"You want to hear the story of Canários?" he asked me. "I knew the place well. Lived in the next village, Lagoa Verde. It can't have been more than a mile away. Some of the settlers had been there for going on twenty years. There were thirty-three families, and they worked communally and lived in one village. One fine day, rancher Palmério rolled up and told them the land belonged to him. He said he wouldn't be troubling them, just thought they'd like to know.

"Things went on all right for a couple of years, and then suddenly he told them they'd have to start paying rent. Of course they didn't agree, so he got an eviction order. The police turned up one morning and ordered everyone out of their houses, made the men kneel down in the hot sun all day, pushed them around. I heard about it so I decided to go along and see what was happening. I didn't tell my wife where I was going! I went over there, and the police pointed their guns at me and accused me of coming in defense of the settlers — which I wasn't, not armed anyway — and made me kneel down with the rest. Well, then they started negotiating. The settlers said they'd leave, but they needed a little time to thresh the rice. They reckoned five days. Some said ten days. Anyway, they got out of there.

"Some days later, I was out on the hill and I saw smoke. They were burning the houses. I saw two men running. I think one of them was in uniform. The whole place burned to the ground, saddest thing you ever saw.

"A few days later, Palmério came along to take a look at the mess he'd made. He even brought his wife along with him to gloat. Of course, the villagers got wind of it. When they heard Palmério had been poking about the ruins of their village, they were just sickened, and started planning to get even with him. They set an ambush and killed the pair of them.

"Of course, the authorities put the blame on Josimo. But it had nothing to do with him. It wasn't even his parish. He knew nothing about it."

The day after Palmério's death, the police picked up thirteen men in the villages of Juverlândia and San José. After being beaten within an inch of his life, one of them said that it had been Josimo's idea. Josimo and Lurdinha.

Two weeks later, they were arrested. Lurdinha told me about it. "There was to be a visit to the area by a group of bishops and representatives from Congress. The commission also included a couple of members of the European Parliament. They were providing funding for the Carajás mining project, and were here to investigate allegations of extreme violence in the area. In the previous three months, the bishops had documented seven deaths, eighty houses burned and six hundred people evicted — all in the

Parrot's Beak. Naturally, the State Secretary for Public Safety had denied it all and challenged the bishops to prove it.

"Josimo and I were organizing the visit, and we were on our way to Imperatriz to meet the commission. We missed the last ferry and so we went back to the house of Raimunda Bezerra in São Miguel. The next morning the police came bursting in at six o'clock. I said to them, 'What's all this about?' and they said, 'We've come to arrest you.' Josimo was still in his hammock. So we took a shower and collected our stuff and they drove us to Itaguatins. They'd already got another four people in jail there.

"I was furious with the police. It was clearly an attempt to upset the visit. They finally moved us down to the military barracks in Araguaina, and kept us there for six days. They didn't beat us up, but it's no picnic being in jail. All of a sudden, they told us we could go. We didn't want to leave because they were still holding the others, but we didn't have much choice.

"One of the workers had been beaten so badly, he said that Josimo and I were responsible for the ambush. He was an old man and he'd been tortured. The police told us he would confirm it, but he told the judge straight out that his confession had been beaten out of him."

I spoke to a couple of the CPT lawyers about the case. Adilar, who was the CPT coordinator at the time, snorted.

"The Canários case was an illegal eviction. Not only illegal but brutal into the bargain. It's not surprising the laborers killed Palmério and his wife after all they'd been through. Naturally the authorities tried to pin it on Josimo. It is true he had meetings with the workers, but nothing more. But the police tried to blame him for the ambush.

"Part of the trouble was the mentality of the landowners. They were of the old-fashioned school, accustomed to having their own way in everything. Then they started to see their influence diminish and they didn't like that. They weren't prepared for the new attitude of the workers, who were beginning to see themselves as people instead of pawns. The landowners blamed it on the CPT and did everything they could to get us out of there.

"We were getting ready for the arrival of a commission consisting of bishops, congressmen and members of the European

Parliament. Josimo and Lurdinha were going to join us in Imperatriz, but they were arrested before they got there. The judge ordered preventive prison over the case of Palmério. There's nothing illegal about that if there's a chance that the accused will run away, but there was clearly no justification in this case. It was a purely political act, to try and upset the commission. We were determined to let them see for themselves what the situation was. We'd scheduled all kinds of demonstrations and meetings, and visits to places like Canários.

"When I arrived at the police station by the ferry to Imperatriz, I was detained too, along with Nicole who happened to be with me. We were held till the afternoon. Nobody seemed to know what to do with us, but there were a lot of accusations flying about. It was all a ploy to hold onto us. Finally, the bishop of Imperatriz intervened and we were released.

"But the visit of the commission went off fine. It started with a closed meeting in Sítio Novo with the union leaders. Then they visited Canários, Camarão, Espírito Santo, Sampaio and Buriti. The authorities did their best to disrupt things, with ostentatious police patrols all over the place, making a lot of noise and bother. It was done purely to create confusion, but the commission could see through that one."

Pedro Luis Dalcero was another lawyer working for the CPT at the time. "You must remember that the police were extremely authoritarian at the time," he told me. "The full force of the law was on the side of the landowners. We're talking '85,'86, before the new constitution. In the cases against the landowners, the authorities would procrastinate in every possible way.

"We told Josimo to deny everything. After all, he didn't participate directly in the ambush. When they questioned him, he said he knew nothing about it, but he did know Palmério had prompted the eviction of thirty-three families from Canários, and he believed that was what lay behind it. He would have done better to keep his mouth shut, but he would never compromise. I don't know how many times I must have told him to use a bit more tact. He never would make any concessions. He could be very trying, sometimes!"

After his release, Josimo was interviewed by *Convívio* magazine, and asked how it felt to be jailed.

"I understood that commitment to Christ and his people requires the courage to face persecution and prison," he answered. "We should be prepared to be arrested in the cause of justice. And the simple fact of being arrested doesn't mean we have done our all for the Kingdom of Heaven. God is the judge of that. Our job is to keep up the fight for justice."

Despite the efforts of the authorities, the visit of the commission was a great success. More than fifteen hundred people attended the demonstration in Axixá, and there was bitter criticism directed against the Goiás State Secretary for Public Security — a man notoriously vindictive towards peasant farmers. The commission was unsuccessful in its attempts to visit Josimo and Lurdinha in prison in Itaguatins, but did manage to contact them later in Araguaina. They paid a visit to Canários. All that remained were the skeletons of the houses, and a few scorched orange trees. Even the goal posts on the football field had been burned. One of the Europeans compared the desolate scene to wartime bombings in Europe. A Brazilian bishop was reminded of the last days of Canudos when ten thousand federal troops had laid siege to a holy man and his followers in the backlands of Bahia.

It was the first time that the ugly realities of the land wars had received international exposure. One thing was rapidly becoming clear, both at home and abroad. The situation in the Parrot's Beak was beginning to look perilously like civil war.

Chapter Seven

Resistance

The story goes that when God made Brazil he gave it everything: abundant sunshine, huge fertile lands, boundless forests, gold, diamonds, and every mineral resource. The other nations looked on in envy and finally complained to God that He was giving Brazil the best of everything. "Ah," said God in His mysterious way. "Just wait till you see the people I am going to put there."

God never explained what He meant, and Brazil ended up with a rainbow-colored people, a people who came from European, African and American Indian stock. The small European population rapidly wiped out most of the Indians, imported Africans to do the work and then proceeded to intermarry and produce children of every hue. They developed a system where a tiny minority preyed off the great majority, and the worm never turned. They lived in a land of massive, shocking inequality, and for five hundred years, they never suffered a major revolution. Then the worm began to turn.

There's plenty to revolt about. In Brazil, the difference between haves and have-nots is greater than in any other country in the world. According to UNDP statistics for 1996, the top twenty percent of Brazilians are 32.1 times richer than the bottom twenty percent. While twelve million rural Brazilians have either no land at all or not enough to live on, the biggest landholding in the country measures 16,686 square miles — over ten and a half million acres. That's bigger than Switzerland, twice the size of Massachusetts. And it's by no means an isolated case. The next seven on the list total, between them, 35,631 square miles. That's the size of Portugal or Indiana. The eighteen biggest landowners have, between them, an area of sixty-nine thousand square miles — the size of Holland, Switzerland and Ireland combined. Towards the bottom of the pile there are three million tiny farms of less than ten acres. And below them, twelve million people who can't make ends meet because they haven't got land.

Similar to the rural depletion suffered by most other countries, there are a lot fewer rural Brazilians than there used to be. These days not more than 25% of the population lives on the land. Between 1960 and 1980 more than twenty-eight million left their lands. Modernization rendered their little plots uncompetitive, the introduction of a money-based economy bankrupted them, mechanization deprived them of the seasonal waged jobs which they needed to supplement their incomes, drought forced them to eat the seed corn, and land-grabbers hustled them out at gunpoint.

Developmental experts have long recognized the benefits to be derived from helping rural people find work where they live, since direct and indirect costs of creating jobs in urban areas are very high. Although there is no conclusive evidence to suggest that large, fully operational farms will produce more if they are divided up into smaller plots, it is certainly true that underutilized lands, once subdivided, will both sustain larger numbers of people and produce better than before. Many of Brazil's largest landholdings are not suitable for intensive cultivation, but there is still plenty of potentially good land that is seriously underexploited, and should be more justly used. In response to trends of urban migration, the continuing concentration of land ownership in the hands of a few, and the increasingly vociferous demands from the landless themselves, the Brazilian government finds it imperative to carry out some form of land redistribution. But fierce pressure from the large landowners, who themselves constitute the majority of those responsible for governing, means that the government has not yet been able to find either the will or the capacity to bring about meaningful changes.

There have been rumblings about land reform in Brazil for fifty years, but nothing significant has ever come of it. Between 1945 and 1964, ninety-odd bills on the subject were presented to Congress. All of them were knocked out by the large landowners. The military government which took over in 1964 passed a Land Statute which paid lip service to the idea of land reform. It included land reform in a package of improved agricultural techniques, credit, marketing and rural infrastructure. All good stuff, but nothing ever actually happened.

Instead of embarking on social reforms, the generals concentrated on a rapid program of industrialization, a meaningless miracle which, for a short time, transformed Brazil into an economic tiger with an astounding annual growth rate of 10%. Falling over themselves to promote growth, the government encouraged the mechanization of the agricultural sector, which led to some impressive export figures.

But export-based growth did not bring overall development, leading instead to a massive foreign debt. The short answer was to print more money, and the resultant inflation rapidly damaged the economy even further.

Worse still, the people were denied any meaningful form of protest. But as the decade of the seventies drew to its close, and it became apparent that the generals couldn't hold onto power forever, pressure began to build up for some serious action on the land problem. The large landowners weren't too concerned because they thought land reform would never happen. The urban middle class, on the other hand, supported the idea of a regenerated rural economy. It would produce markets for consumer goods, and improved agricultural production could only benefit everybody. The rapid industrialization of São Paulo spun off some labor leaders, and one of them, Luis Inácio da Silva, known to everyone as Lula, founded the Workers' Party, the PT. For the first time urban workers found themselves with a voice, and they lost no time in pressing for improved working conditions and salaries. They also supported the rural poor, and here their main focus was for fairer land distribution. So the peasants suddenly found they had a support base, and as the land wars heated up in the 1980s the church, the unions, and the PT all weighed in to encourage them to sit tight on their lands.

By law they could acquire squatters' rights by living and working on unused land for a year and a day. The landowners and land-grabbers were aware of this and did all they could to make sure that it didn't happen. The peasants and their supporters did all they could to make sure it did. And so it was that even in the distant reaches of Northern Goiás, even in the Parrot's Beak, squatters began to organize themselves to stay and fight for their lands. And it frightened the wits out of the landowners.

In the village of Sete Barracas, I heard the story of one community's fight for the land. I had trudged five miles from the road and was glad to sit down on a pile of logs beside a group of women. It was a hot lazy afternoon, someone was rhythmically pounding corn, and the children were playing in the dirt outside the school. Hermília told me their story. An attractive woman of about fifty, she was dressed in a faded blue skirt, tee shirt and flip-flops.

"This used to be a wonderful place," she smiled at me. "We all worked together, we grew more rice than we could eat. It was a land of plenty. Then in 1973, we heard that some politician or other had bought our land. His foreman was called Joâo Cardoso, and the moment I set eyes on him I knew he was a bad lot. First of all, he started to clear the forest to make fences. Then he told us to keep out, and finally he told us we'd have to leave. There was nobody to advise us, and we didn't have the nerve to stay on, not after he sent those *pistoleiros* around. My father-in-law told me there was nothing we could do, and my husband told me they'd take all our land. They said we could keep twenty-one acres. We had a hundred and fifty.

"One day the foreman said to us, 'You can't come in here any more because we're going to put in a fence.' Well, we'd never seen fences round here. He said we'd better stay off the land, and we'd better not plant any more rice either because the land belonged to him.

"So there we were, living right next to all that land and we couldn't use it. What could we do? We couldn't feed our families. We were going to have to figure something out.

"The owner of the place never set foot here. He lived in Araguaina. The only one here was the foreman. We had to do something. We weren't going to die of hunger. So thirteen families sneaked in, made clearings in the forest, and planted rice, manioc and beans. We were expecting trouble, but nothing happened. The next season, a few more families joined us, and still the foreman did nothing. Then suddenly he sent a message that anyone who went in there would be killed. By that time, we were fifty-two families, and we all had our fields planted up. We didn't live on the land, of course, but it was all planted up. Thirty acres of it.

"We had a mass of stuff planted: rice, vegetables, corn, beans and manioc. Then one day they came in with an eviction order and told us we all had to leave. They said it was their land. They made us move our houses too, because they knew if we stayed put, we'd go in again. They threw us all out, along with all our stuff, chickens, pigs, the lot.

"What were we to do? There was the land all planted up. The foreman started sowing grass on top of our crops. I remember he said to us, 'Up till now you've been working on this land, and I've stayed out of it. From now, on it's going to be different. I'm going to be working on the land and you're going to be staying off it. If you do come in, I'm not responsible for what happens.'

"One week after the eviction, João Cardoso sent in a bunch of *pistoleiros* to live in one of the houses that used to be ours. They came in with a truck covered with a tarpaulin and underneath, it was stuffed with arms. Boxes and boxes of ammunition.

"So we couldn't get to our fields, and we had completely run out of food. We didn't have a thing to eat, but no one had the nerve to go in. After all, no one wants to die... But we were hungry. So I said, 'Let's go in and collect some babassu nuts. Then at least we'll have something to sell.'

"You know how we crack the babassu, don't you? We collect them up into a pile, then we sit on the floor like this." She slid gracefully onto the ground with one leg crooked in front of her. "We hold an ax blade with our feet, we place the nut on the blade and then we smash down with a stone. It cracks clean when you've got the knack of it. Anyway, as I was saying, my sister and I went in that day, and we took a large dog with us. We had to go right by the house, and there was a *pistoleiro* lying in a hammock. When he saw us, he fired a couple of shots in the air. The dog ran away, and my sister said, 'Let's go back.' But I said, 'No, let's go on.' So we did — not that we collected a lot of babassu that day— we can't have got more than a canful. But the next day, we went back in and got some more.

"It's the only place around here that's got babassu, so we kept sneaking back. One day we ran slap into the foreman. A big man he was, but we went up to him anyway. We told him we needed to collect some babassu, and he told us we couldn't. But we kept on. We had to live on something.

"The *pistoleiros* were living in one of the houses. There wasn't much for them to do, so they used to drink a lot, and shoot at bottles or mangoes for target practice. Then on January 15th, something wonderful happened. They all went to another house to watch TV, and left a candle burning on top of a cardboard box. The house was full of arms: revolvers, rifles, and boxes and boxes of ammunition. Well, that candle burnt and burnt and then ... the house caught fire! All the ammunition started to explode. It sounded just like a shoot-out. I remember I was in my mother's house and I said to her, 'What on earth is all that noise?' And she said, 'The foreman's house is on fire.'

"We were all terrified they'd blame us for it, but the foreman admitted he'd been the one who left the candle burning. Then we got to thinking that things would get better because the *pistoleiros* didn't have any weapons left. They'd kept us out of the fields, and the rice was just about ready to harvest. Thirty acres of rice -- we weren't about to let them steal it all. My husband went to look and see what was going on, and sure enough, there they were harvesting it! So that decided us. We took twenty-three men with us, and we went up to the *pistoleiros* and told them it was our rice and they'd better push off. They said they'd go halves with us, but we said we wanted it all. When the foreman saw our twenty-three men, he went white with fear. He wasn't armed that day, he was only wearing shorts. So we said, 'Up to now you have been the boss round here, but from now on it's going to be us. We're the ones who are going to harvest the rice.' That gave him a nasty shock! He asked us if he could take the rice he'd already threshed, and we agreed because we thought it couldn't have been very much. Then we found he'd threshed a lot! But we kept our word. Next day we got every able-bodied member of the community, men, women and children, and we marched in and told the *pistoleiros* to get out. 'No one is going to harvest one more stalk of rice,' we said. We worked all day and got a sackful each. And then we got to thinking: there's a lot more rice to harvest. So we'll go in again. but in a group, because if we go singly they may try to get us. We all got together and harvested the lot, stored it and divided it among us. Some other communities sent as many as twenty people to help us.

"The incredible thing was that the *pistoleiros* never showed their faces here again. We couldn't believe it at first, but as time went on we began to feel safer and safer. By May 1986, nothing had happened, no threats, no *pistoleiros*. So we moved back in onto the land. And, thank the Lord, we are still here to this day!"

The peasants' organized political resistance began with a demonstration scheduled for June 23rd, 1984, in Augustinópolis, the seat of the local ranchers' association. Six thousand people gathered in the town square to denounce the land situation. They wanted the world to know that they were being thrown off their lands. They wanted to shame the authorities into supporting them. They wanted to put a stop to violence by the police and *pistoleiros*. They wanted to have free access to the babassu trees, traditionally considered common property. Most of all, they wanted the government to come through on its promises of land reform. They were backed by union representatives at the local and national level, the CPT, the base communities of the church, and the Workers' Party. They even invited a federal deputy, Irma Passoni, from São Paulo.

One of their chief complaints was about GETAT, the military body created by the government to oversee land settlement in the area, whose strategy was to keep the peace — which occasionally involved rapid resettlement of peasants out of disputed areas of land. The responses of the authorities to conflict were erratic and unpredictable, and the peasants lived in mortal fear of GETAT, alleging that it treated them with extreme disrespect and violence.

Among the people most intimately involved in teaching the peasants about their political rights was Sister Lurdinha. She was such a fervent campaigner that she even left her religious order in order to run for elective office in the Workers' Party. I asked her to tell me something about GETAT.

"It was an extraordinarily powerful group," she told me. "They actually had more power than the president of the republic, because of the National Security Laws. That meant they reported directly to the National Security Council in Brasília and they could suspend civil rights and things like that. GETAT always sided with the police. Although they did give out some land titles to the peasants, it was really done to keep them quiet. Basically, they were on the side of the big boys. I remember once going to an eviction with Josimo. It was at a place called São Felix. When we got there, we found a couple of ranchers and a bunch of military policemen all armed with machine guns, who had arrived in the GETAT car. The first thing they'd done had been to lock up a whole lot of the villagers inside one of the houses. During that day, we saw children who had been beaten up, workers made to crawl like animals, blood everywhere. GETAT was behind it all.

"One of the things that happened that day at Augustinópolis was that we burned GETAT in effigy. There was a lot of discussion in the CPT about that. Most people considered it too provocative, but Josimo supported us. He said that we'd never had the chance to express our feelings in such a way before, and he wasn't going to be the one to stop us."

The peasants had been preparing their demonstration for almost a year, so it didn't come as a surprise to the local ranchers and the town authorities. But they hadn't expected such numbers, and to start with, they kept quiet. They stood around in little knots, grumbling and threatening to disrupt events. At first, it seemed that they would leave it at that.

In the afternoon, there was a procession to the main square where there were speeches, songs, and poetry — outpourings of people's rage and grief at their dispossession. Elated by such a tangible demonstration of solidarity, Josimo took the mike and said to the crowd, "You see that man standing there? Well, he's the sheriff. Those men next to him are the *pistoleiros* and I want you all to take a good look at them. They're here to frighten us." The *pistoleiros* squirmed as six thousand pairs of eyes turned in their direction.

Tension had been smoldering all day, and the first signs of trouble came when town councilman Nenem and his brother Nenezão suddenly burst into the square in their car and drove round honking their horn, clearly hoping to stir up trouble. Irma Passoni, the federal deputy, went up to them and asked them what they thought they were doing. Nenem started blustering that he was a councilman, to which Irma Passoni retorted that she was from the federal government. If he had something to say, she informed him brusquely, he could get up on stage and say it. Tempers rose, and some of the bystanders started rocking the car. Nenem beat a noisy retreat to the nearest bar, and the square was barricaded to avoid further trouble.

The business of the day was nearly done, so the organizers decided to quit while they were ahead. They instructed the workers to get into their trucks and leave all together, to forestall any problems. But there was one man, Vitorino Bandeira Barros, who couldn't resist the chance to stop off at a bar for a pack of cigarettes. As luck would have it, he chose the bar where Nenem and his friends were drinking, and it wasn't long before a scuffle broke out. Insults started flying, and Nenezão seized a chair and flung it at Vitorino. Without a word, Vitorino whipped out his knife and Nenezão fell to the ground in a pool of blood.

The news got round in a flash. Within minutes, a hostile crowd had gathered and advanced on the square where the organizers were clearing up. The crowd rained stones on the cars, and things looked very ugly indeed. Fortunately the military police were on hand, and after some heated discussion, most of the organizers managed to get away. As the last of them scurried to collect the sound equipment, they were surrounded by a jeering mob led by Nenem. He had finally found the excuse he had been waiting for all day, and he was determined to avenge the blood of Nenezão. The mob charged, screaming insults. "Terrorists!" they yelled, "Murderers!" The men fingered their guns, itching for an excuse to kill someone.

Josimo ran to the police station to seek police protection. The sheriff laughed in his face. "You've got a nerve!" he told him. "You're the one who deserves to be arrested."

Two more cars managed to leave, and the last four organizers dived into the room where they had stored their remaining pieces of equipment. Just as they were staggering out the door with cardboard boxes full of pamphlets, banners, loudspeakers, coffee flasks and the rest of their paraphernalia, the mob stormed the house. A police car appeared and slowly circled the square, then beat a prudent retreat.

The situation looked irretrievable. "I thought we'd had it," said one of CPT staff afterwards. "Never been so frightened in my life. I was convinced they were going to lynch us. And you'll never believe how we got out of it. Itamar, from the Brazilian Democratic Movement Party, a middle-of-the-road sort of guy, the last person you'd have expected to come to our rescue, faced the crowd and told them straight that Nenezão had always been a bad lot, and there was no way they could hold us responsible for his death. He said it was Nenezão who had attacked Vitorino in the first place, and that it was our democratic right to get together and discuss things, that they ought to be grateful we could do it, after so many years of military government. Then he turned to me and said 'Beat it! Quick!' and so we did. My God, that was a lucky escape.

"The funny thing was," he continued, "That while we were all together, we were stronger than they were. They knew it and we knew it. Then suddenly, the situation was reversed. Instead of being 6,000, we were just a handful, in a hostile town surrounded by *pistoleiros* with a dead man in their midst. The sheriff laughed when we went to see him — he wanted at least one death on our side to even things out."

The peasants had had their moment of glory. But it didn't change anything. Five months later, they sent a document to the government in Brasília with a copy to the bishops. They wanted to emphasize that nothing had changed — if anything, things had gotten worse. The figures they cited told their grim tale. Since that day in Augustinópolis, 140 families had been thrown off their land, 115 houses had been burned, 18 people had been beaten up, 13 more had been seized by the police and two were in jail. Countless people had been threatened with death.

They placed the blame squarely on GETAT, the federal and military police, the large landowners and the local politicians. They said that their families were living in a state of fear, never knowing what the next day would bring, when the next houses would be burned, when the next eviction would come, when the next men would be kidnapped, arrested, interrogated and tortured. How were they to respond? Should they meet violence with violence?

I pondered that as I read their document, and then I asked a couple of union leaders what they thought. Joâo Custódio didn't hesitate. "There's two things here," he grinned at me. "First of all what it says in the Bible. 'Thou shalt not kill.' That's quite right, because violence is a thing that has no end. It doesn't solve anything."

"Because it generates more violence?" I asked.

"Yes," he answered, dragging on his palm leaf cigarette. "But there is one point. If you attack an animal, it will defend itself. A steer will toss you. A pig will bite you. So a man will react, not because he wants violence, but to defend himself. And because he knows he won't get any help from the authorities. They don't see us laborers as human beings, you see. They don't think of us as Christians. Quite the opposite. They go after us, and that's where violence comes in."

"So we can't blame the settler who takes the law into his own hands?" I asked.

"No, we can't," he said. "The Bible says that he who doesn't have a sword should buy one. I think we need arms to defend ourselves. Either you fight or you die."

Maria Senhora was equally straightforward. "It's not easy," she told me with a big smile. "I think this: if someone comes to kill me and I kill him first, I believe that he is the one to blame. He began it, he wanted to take my life, and if he got killed it's his own fault. If someone comes to kill me, of course I'll kill him if I can. I wouldn't consider that I was a murderer. I'd say that he killed himself, because he was the one with murder in his heart. I don't think God will hold me responsible."

"And was that day at Augustinópolis the beginning of the end for Josimo?" I asked them.

"I think it was," said Maria Senhora, sadly. "Because that day was the first time they realized that we meant business. They'd never really understood how desperate we were. Desperate people will do anything to defend their families, and in the end they will always win."

Her words reminded me of a poem I had recently read. It came from Guatemala, a nation well versed in the ways of repression. Here's how it goes:

> You have a gun
> And I am hungry.
>
> You have a gun
> because
> I am hungry.
>
> You have a gun
> therefore
> I am hungry.
>
> You can have a gun,
> You can have a thousand bullets, and even
> another thousand,
> You can waste them all on my poor body,
> You can kill me, one, two, three, two thousand,
> seven thousand times,
> but in the long run
> I will always be better armed than you
> if you have a gun
> and I
> only hunger.

Chapter Eight

Friends and Enemies

São Sebastião was the seat of Josimo's parish and the seat of local government. But the place where he was most loved — and most hated — was the village of Buriti.

It's larger than São Sebastião. These days, it has become a town in its own right, and the new mayor is João Olímpio, formerly deputy mayor of São Sebastião, and sworn enemy to Josimo. The town has a few paved streets in the center, a bus station, a telephone cabin, a pleasant little hotel, a school, a hospital and a cheese factory that sends cheese to Fortaleza, 700 miles away.

The CPT people told me to go to Mara's house. A neat little house, it boasted more furniture than most — several uncomfortable wooden chairs covered with rag mats, a dresser with an elderly black and white television, a treadle sewing machine and lots of crochet mats everywhere. The walls were rough mud, except for the bedrooms which had crude wooden partitions. I shared a room with Judith and Virginia, seventeen and fifteen years old, and both ravishingly pretty. They had a bed each, and there was just room for me to sling a hammock in between.

Mara couldn't tell me enough about Josimo. "Josimo?" she said, smiling. "He was a great friend. A wonderful person, he was. He always kept his cool, no matter what happened. He used to share in every part of our lives. I remember he used to come with us to the fields, walking through the mud. He didn't care. He was different, not at all like the sort of priest we were used to.

"I don't believe I ever saw him angry. He was always ready to help out, whatever the problem was. I don't know why so many people were opposed to him, because he'd have given you the shirt off his back. He worked with Lurdinha and the Sisters, and the ranchers used to say they were inciting us to invade the land, but that wasn't true. They were the invaders — we were already on the land. All Josimo did was to tell us to go back in after the evictions. And he arrived in the nick of time, because things were getting very tough for us. If it hadn't been for him, we'd never have had the guts to stick it out. He explained things to us, you see, and told us about our rights. We stayed on the land because we didn't have any place else to go, but it was Josimo who showed us what to do.

"Josimo had lots of enemies. The man who's mayor now, João Olímpio, still can't stand to hear his name. And lots of others hated him: the politicians, the ranchers, even some of the workers. They thought it all wrong that Josimo should preach the Gospel and talk about the land; they'd have preferred him to talk about Heaven. But if you live in the real world, you have to talk about real things. For us, the land is the most important thing of all."

"We had a good fight over the land, let me tell you," put in her husband, João Ananias. "We came here in '69 from the state of Piauí. My brother told me there was a lot of land here that didn't belong to anyone. It was pretty much all forest in those days. We used to go in and start clearing wherever we liked. We had to cut our way in. We cleared and burned the land, we three brothers together, and we built our houses here in this settlement. The land was good. We could grow anything we wanted. We had pigs, everything. Things went fine up to '75.

"That was the year we heard there was trouble over at the village of Campestre. They said it was being claimed by a man called Belisário Rodrigues da Cunha. He burned down an entire village – seventy houses! He even knocked the chapel down. We heard about it but we kept quiet. After all, it was long way away, and we were doing OK.

"In '76, our turn came. We were in the fields one day and suddenly a big bunch of men came in and told us we'd have to get out. They said it wasn't our land and that we'd better leave if we didn't want any trouble. Well, I said, 'Come on, fellows, we can't leave this place. It's our land. We cleared it. Everything we have is here.'

"They went away, but next day they were back with the police, and then we found we were in deep trouble. The police said the land didn't belong to us, we didn't have title to it and we'd have to go. They said we could take out the harvest and the new owner would compensate us.

"Well, after they'd gone away, we didn't know what to do. We finally decided to sit tight for a bit, just to see what would happen. Then the *pistoleiros* started coming round, threatening to burn the houses and rape the women. At that point, we all cleared out and came back to the village."

"Did you have a place to stay?" I asked.

"Yes we did," said João, "We had our houses in the village. What we had on the land was more like a little shelter: somewhere to cook lunch, get out of the rain or store the rice, that sort of thing. Sometimes we'd sleep there for a night or two if we were working late in the fields. It was after we'd come back to the village that we heard the police were after my Dad. He ran for it and hid here with us. They couldn't find him for several days, but in the end they picked him up, and made him sign some document or other. He couldn't read, of course, but they told him it was an indemnity. They said it was worth 7000 cruzeiros, and he was lucky to get it. After he'd signed, they explained that he couldn't go onto the land any more.

"That was just about the time the CPT people had turned up, and when they heard what was going on they sent a lawyer to talk with us and tell us what to do. He spent a week with us. I remember he said, 'Well, people, if you won't go back on to the land, how can I help you? You fight on the land, and I'll fight in the courts." And then he said, 'You get back to work and look out for yourselves. If you have to hide, hide. If a *pistoleiro* comes after you, kill him.'

"Then the bishop came up to see what was going on," added Mara. "Dom Aloísio, the same bishop we've got now. He'd heard how bad things were up here, and he wanted to see for himself. João and I walked in with him and we took pictures. They'd burned the shelters with all the rice in them —100 sacks— and they burned our fields too. So we couldn't go back, we had nothing to eat and nowhere to plant our crops."

"We did go back, though," said João. "One day my brother and I decided we weren't going to stand for it another day. We had nothing left. They'd given us a bit of money — we had to go after them twice before we got it — but it wasn't worth anything when we did get it. We couldn't stand to see the place going to ruin — all that cane, potatoes, manioc, bananas. We went in again, and we all worked together. It was safer that way.

"In '83, some of the *pistoleiros* got into a fight with each other. We don't know exactly how it happened, but two or three of them died. That led to all sorts of trouble, as you can imagine. Lots of people were indicted, including me and my brother. GETAT came here and held a meeting in the school. They said they'd come to sort things out; we thought that was the end of us. We couldn't believe our ears when they said we could go back onto the land, and that we were the legal owners. They promised to protect us. They fenced the place and told the rancher he wasn't to cross the fence line. After that, the *pistoleiros* never troubled us again."

"So it was a happy ending?" I inquired.

"Yes," answered João. "But they never did survey the land, and we never got our titles. It'll be ten years next month, and we still haven't got them."

"Of course it was a great thing," said Mara. "But without the titles, we still feel insecure. We're afraid that the place might end up in the hands of the ranchers anyway because it's never been surveyed. The government people keep saying they'll do it, but they come here in the rainy season and then they complain that they can't get in to do the survey. I don't know how it is that they can't get in, since we go in all the time!

"Josimo used to say that everyone should have a piece of land to plant what he needed to feed himself. Of course, the ranchers didn't like that. They want us to be dependent on them all our lives. Josimo said we're all children of God, and God is our father. No father wants some of his children to be very rich and have everything they want while the others are poor and have nothing. A father wants all his children to have a decent life. God didn't make the earth and say, "All right. The ranchers can have it all and the rest can have nothing." He made the earth for all of us. But Josimo made himself a lot of enemies talking that way."

One of them was the new mayor, João Olímpio. In Josimo's day, he was deputy mayor to Zé Carneiro, but now his time has come, and he has just moved into a grand rented house, which boasts a tiled floor, a large color television and a parabolic antenna. I chatted to his wife, Toninha, a small dark woman who was buying yards of lace. She is accustomed to receiving large numbers of people to ask favors, and I took my place meekly in the line. I had to go there three times before I caught the mayor; it was Carnival and he had hired a band which rent the night air with its deafening sambas (and cost, I heard later, half the annual municipal budget). I finally tracked him down one morning after he'd had an all-night session, and the prefect, adorned with several days' growth of beard, was sitting wanly in front of a plate of gristly meat and manioc flour. He waved me to a seat at the table. I helped myself liberally to coffee and corn cakes.

We moved out later onto the airy veranda, and he surrounded himself with tough-looking henchmen. I asked him about rural violence.

"It's always been reported incorrectly," he smiled at me blandly. "It was all the fault of the church. When Padre Josimo got here, he started putting the people up to all sorts of tricks. Land invasions for one. Naturally the ranchers reacted strongly. They had bought the land, and there was the church promoting all sorts of violence and confusion.

"There's a man round here, name of João Japonês. The invaders caused such havoc on his place that he decided to buy them off. He paid them all compensation, but in the end he finally had to negotiate with GETAT and 5000 acres were expropriated for the invaders. 125 families moved in on the land, but today there are only 10 left. They all sold up. That's what happens, you see. They invade other people's property, acquire the land and then sell up. They become professional invaders. Don't go away with the impression that they're lily-white, these people. They'll go in, they'll kill the cattle, burn the fences, sometimes they'll ambush the ranchers. They'll tell lies about how long they've been in there, so that they can acquire squatters' rights. They'll get the land expropriated and then they'll sell up and start again.

"And the church supports them. It's very wrong. Unchristian, I call it. As for the church backing the Workers' Party... This does nothing but promote class division. Such a thing never used to exist. When I was at school, the fathers used to preach the Gospel and ask us to fight against communism. These days they've changed completely. And it does them no good. People are leaving the church all the time. Just look how the evangelical churches are growing.

"Things did get better after Josimo's death, I must say. The church became less radical. The trouble with Josimo was that he never accepted the middle class. Padre Stanislau used to love everyone, but Josimo only cared for the poor. He used to say that theirs was the kingdom of heaven!

"Things have settled down a lot, since. What you see here nowadays isn't violence. It's poverty. And there's a lot of nonsense talked about *pistoleiros*. It's true they did exist at one time, because the police couldn't protect the lives and property of the ranchers, so they had to take the law into their own hands. But all that was in the past. Things are quite different these days. There aren't any *pistoleiros* any more."

I knew for a fact that wasn't true. One of the most notorious enemies of Josimo was a *pistoleiro* called Deca. He still lives in Buriti and it's common knowledge that he still practices his profession.

Deca is brother to Nenem, the councilman from São Sebastião. He is also brother to Nenezão, the one who got killed the day they had the demonstration in Augustinópolis. He was mixed up in the plot to kill Josimo. I was determined to take a look at him.

Mara was nervous about this idea. "None of us go near him," she said anxiously. "We don't even like to go past his house. You'll have to be very careful."

How was I going to talk to him? He was known to dislike journalists, and foreigners even worse. I didn't want to cause any trouble for Mara and her family. And he certainly wouldn't want to talk to me if he had any inkling that I was investigating the case of Josimo.

It was Sister Lurdinha who suggested the way out. "What you could do," she told me, "is go and talk to his neighbor Hugo, the surveyor. Ask Hugo about the land situation, and just play it by ear. Hugo and Deca are thick as thieves, and maybe you can figure out a way to persuade Hugo to take you over there."

So I made my way down the long rutted road to Hugo's house. Hugo has been in Buriti since 1971. After a lengthy, rambling conversation about land titling, he suggested taking me to visit his neighbor. "Deca has been here for years," he said. "He'll tell you about these squabbles over the land."

We walked amicably over to Deca's house. It was a stifling hot afternoon, without a breath of wind, and Deca's place was an inferno. It was full of young men lounging about, chewing chicken bones. We sat on a torn plastic sofa and Hugo muttered to Deca,

"This is an English journalist. She wants to know about the land problems here." He lowered his voice and I could just catch him saying, "She isn't one of them."

Deca looked the part to perfection. He was wearing pointed boots and spurs, a large ornate belt, and he looked as if he'd have you for breakfast with no qualms at all. I took refuge in the elaborate courtesies of the Portuguese language, and hoped I didn't look as apprehensive as I felt.

"People talk a lot of nonsense about the Parrot's Beak," he told me with a big smile. "From the newspapers, you'd think people went around shooting each other all the time. It's a lot more peaceful here than it is in Rio de Janeiro, let me tell you.

"We used to have the occasional spot of bother, but it was all the fault of that communist priest who went around telling people to invade the ranches and causing all sorts of problems. Naturally, the ranchers had to do something about it. A man's got the right to defend his property, hasn't he? Not just a right, it's a moral duty.

"So, they had this spot of bother, and in the end, the invaders managed to get some of the land expropriated — and then what happened? They couldn't get it to grow anything. I don't suppose they're growing a tenth of what they could be. We have to import most of our food from São Paulo.

"The truth of the matter is that people round these parts are a lot of lazy good-for-nothings. You can take Deca's word for it. Deca knows best. Any time you want to come over and see my place, I'll show you how much these people are worth. Lazy buggers, that's what they are. They won't plant, won't lift a finger. You have to give them a damn good kick to get them to do anything at all, and that's God's truth."

Chapter Nine

The Tale of the Telephone

"Bia," I said, as we sat over enormous bowls of milky coffee, in her house in Mulatos, "Tell me about the case of the telephone. What really happened?"

"That wretched telephone?" laughed Bia. "It's been the bane of our lives, and we're still not free of it. It was like this. It was the time of the annual saint's day festival in Buriti, Josimo had a lot of work on his hands and he asked us to go over and help him out for a couple of days. That was when we first heard they were going to build the telephone exchange right next to the church. The first Josimo got to hear about it was when the building crew showed up to start work.

"'Hang on,' he said to the foreman, 'That's church property.'

"'I don't know anything about that,' said the foreman, 'But I got my orders.'

"Josimo went straight to the town hall in São Sebastião to look up the land records. He had to type out the document himself, since there was no one else available. There wasn't a title deed — they're not that efficient in these parts — but the donation of the land had been recorded in the registry. So Josimo copied it out and the chairman signed it. At least we had some proof that the land belonged to the parish. It would have been a very bad place to build; it was right next to the church.

"When Josimo got back, they'd already started on the foundations. The posts and string were in place to mark it up. Josimo was so indignant that he asked the foreman to stop work immediately. As it happens, Joâo Olímpio, the deputy mayor at the time, was there — now he's the mayor. Josimo read out the document to him very politely, and asked if they could stop. But Joâo Olímpio wouldn't hear of such a thing. Then he started shouting at Josimo, calling him names, saying that he was a bad influence on the people, and goodness knows what besides. He simply wouldn't listen to reason. I got so mad I went ahead and yanked out the posts and the string. I couldn't stand it any longer. Joâo Olímpio stormed off, but we could tell that wasn't the last of it.

"We went to Lurdinha's house and shortly afterwards Zé Carneiro, the mayor, came roaring up with Nego Chaves the policeman, demanding to talk to Josimo. It was a Saturday, Josimo was going to do a baptism at 3 o'clock, and the church was full of people. They went to the bottom of the garden and stayed there a long time, almost an hour. Then we thought: the church is full of people and we can't leave them all sitting there."

"So I thought: I'll go and talk to them," said Mada. "And I said, 'Excuse me, but it's 3 o'clock. There's a baptism and the church is full.' I heard Zé Carneiro say, 'Look, I'm going ahead with this; I'll show you who's the boss round here. If necessary, I'll call in 200 policemen.'

"Josimo just smiled and said, 'You know best.' Then Zé Carneiro rounded on me and said we were upsetting his work, causing discontent among the teachers and turning them all against him. It's true the teachers were always miserably paid, always three or four months late. We used to give them all the support we could, and as a result they were forbidden to go to church. The mayor told them if they set foot in the church, they'd be fired."

"Well," said Bia, "Next day the councilmen sent some representatives to talk to us to see if we could come to a compromise. And I believe we might have been able to work something out. So we agreed to discuss it on Wednesday.

"On the Monday morning at 11 o'clock, a neighbor came running to Lurdinha's house and said, 'Quick! Turn on the radio. National Radio.' And there was Zé Carneiro talking about Josimo and calling him a communist and a terrorist. On national radio! He was saying terrible things about Josimo and Lurdinha. After that, we decided there was no way we could dialogue with him. Here we had already agreed to a meeting, and there he was, going behind our backs in that sneaky way!

"We decided we couldn't leave things at that. We told Josimo he'd have to refute what Zé Carneiro had said. We tried and tried to get radio time for Josimo, but they wouldn't give it to him. Josimo promised he wouldn't enter into controversy, he simply wanted to clarify the situation. They said it was forbidden to criticize the authorities on national radio.

"We couldn't get any further than that because we all had to go to a Bible course in Tocantinópolis which lasted for two weeks. One of the men from Buriti came down and told us that the telephone exchange was ready for roofing, and the people were furious. Since Zé Carneiro said it was Dom Aloísio, the bishop, who had authorized the building in the first place, we decided to confront him. We marched into Dom Aloísio's room and asked him what the story was. He told us he had discussed it with the mayor, but they hadn't come to any conclusion and it must have been a misunderstanding. We really leaned hard on the poor man, and finally he said he'd go to Buriti the following week to sort it out. So we sent a message to tell the community to wait for the bishop."

"So what was happening all that time in Buriti?" I asked Joâo Ananias later.

"Well," said Joâo, "None of us wanted the blessed telephone anyway. And Zé Carneiro could have put it any place he wanted. He didn't have to put it on church land."

"He did it purely to upset Josimo," said Joâo. "He wanted to prove who was boss. Josimo didn't see it that way; he saw it as an attempt to coerce the church. We went there when they were measuring it up. We said, 'Don't do it,' and they said, 'Sure we are going to do it.' We said, 'You can't. It's church land.' But they didn't pay any attention to that.

"So we decided to go to the town council in São Sebastião. The man in charge there looked up in his book and he found the record of the meeting when they donated that land to the church."

"So you had a document to prove it?" I asked.

"Yes we did," said Joâo. "All measured up, so many yards here, bordering X here and Y there. It was all properly done. We showed the document to the foreman, and he said he didn't care, he was going ahead anyway. They were digging the foundations, and they didn't even stop to listen.

"The Sisters were with us, and Bia got so mad she started pulling up the markers. Then the deputy mayor, Joâo Olímpio, showed up and said, 'You can't do that. If you don't get out of here now, I can't answer for the consequences.'

"There was no end of trouble after that. They blocked off the square. There was one woman who was a crony of the mayor, Zé

Carneiro, and she got into her car and went over to São Sebastião to get him. He came steaming up and said, 'Where's that Padre Josimo got to?'

"'He's in Lurdinha's house,' we told him. 'Would you like us to take you there?'

"'I can find my own way,' he said. So he went there, and found Josimo sitting in the garden. A whole crowd of people went along with the mayor, including a *pistoleiro*. We went along too, and we didn't like the look of it at all. They were all armed. When Zé Carneiro left, I heard him say, 'That padre will have to go.'

"The next day Josimo left for Tocantinópolis."

"He was away for fifteen days," said Mara, "doing the Bible course."

"They seized their opportunity and built the telephone exchange..."

"Worked on it night and day..."

"Had it almost finished..."

"All but the roofing..."

"And that was when we decided to knock the building down," finished Joâo. "We tried to get through to Tocantinópolis on the phone, but we couldn't talk freely because the operator, one of Zé Carneiro's stooges, was listening in. So we sent somebody down to tell Josimo what was going on. Josimo spoke to the bishop and the bishop said he'd come and talk to the mayor."

"But we never trusted that bishop," said Mara. "We thought he'd sell us down the river. So we decided to do it before he came."

"Was it over there?" I said, pointing to the church.

"Yes," said Mara, "Where that little house is."

"You were here. You saw them building it," I said. "What did you think?"

"We saw them building it all right," said Joâo. "It made us very angry. But we couldn't do anything. They barricaded the square and put police on the corners. There were *pistoleiros* hanging about everywhere, and lots of people in the village were working on the building. Working for free! Well, it was all too much for us, so one day we went there and knocked it down."

"What did the police do?" I asked. "Were they there?"

"No," he answered. "It was at night. They'd left."

"We'd got it all set up," said Mara. "Blocked off the square, stood guard, and stopped the traffic. We had to provide some security because we didn't want any trouble. So a big group of people went there... "

"And suddenly it was like a great wind, and — pronto — the building came down," grinned Joâo.

"It didn't take much time?" I asked.

"No time at all," said Joâo. "Not even fifteen minutes. And afterwards, there wasn't a soul in the place. Everyone vanished and that was it."

"And Josimo wasn't even there?" I asked.

"That's right," he told me.

"What about the story of the Sisters carrying machine-guns?" I pursued.

"All lies," said Mara succinctly. "They weren't here either."

"So you organized it all yourselves?" I asked.

"That's right," Joâo nodded his head vigorously. "The Sisters had nothing to do with it, and Josimo didn't either. And as for the story about Lurdinha with a machine-gun, it's all nonsense. We did it ourselves. We didn't want the damned telephone exchange on church land."

"So what were the repercussions?" I asked.

"The first thing was silence," said Mara. "Complete silence. Such a silence that you could hear your heart beat. Everyone bolted themselves inside their houses and kept their heads down — *Ave Maria!* Even the next day, no-one talked about it, only inside their houses."

"What did the police do?" I inquired.

"Nothing," she answered. "They had no proof."

"The Federal Police came in pretty damn quick!" Joâo told me. "They kept sniffing about until they found a lead. Beat a few people up. One of the lads was poking about in the ruins and the police happened to get a picture of him. The sheriff picked him up and beat the daylights out of him. And he turned us all in."

"A few months later we were summonsed," Bia told me. "Josimo, Lurdinha, Mada and I. Mada was away at the time, but I was called to Tocantinópolis by the regional police chief. I went with Josimo and Lurdinha, and we were all interrogated. They took a mass of photos and fingerprints. The chief of police asked me who had knocked down the telephone exchange. He was so rude that I told him I wasn't going to answer. He told me he'd heard we were trafficking children, showing subversive films and running a guerrilla training camp up in the forest. I burst out laughing when I heard that, and that made him madder than ever. There were five witnesses, one of the bus drivers, one of Deca's brothers, Sergeant Mendes, and two others. Later on, three dropped out and two were left, Mendes and Davi. They said they'd seen us there with machine-guns, but they couldn't have seen anything at all that night because there was a power cut!

"I heard the other day that the witnesses are fed up because the whole thing is dragging on so long. Whenever they set a date for a hearing, they cancel it at the last minute, or the judge doesn't show up. So they've said they aren't going to testify. It's not as if they saw anything, anyway!"

The document that proves church ownership of the land refers to the fifth session of the São Sebastião town council, and is dated December 22nd, 1980. The witnesses made the following statements to the State Secretary for Public Security on July 12th 1984:

Sergeant Antônio Mendes Costa of the military police said that Josimo led the group that moved the markers of the foundations. He also testified that the nuns were carrying machine-guns, and that Josimo had hired a bus to bring in people to knock the building down. He stated that afterwards they all went off to celebrate, and that the following day Josimo drove round the square with a group of armed workers.

Isaias, the dentist, stated that he was asked by Zé Carneiro to keep an eye on the building. On July 30th, he was told he could go home because they were going to come to an agreement. He later heard that Josimo had knocked the building down. He saw armed men outside João Olímpio's house and ran to warn him, only to find out that he had left town.

Raimundo Nonato Costa, shopkeeper, was out of town at the time and returned to hear the news. He heard they were trying to kill João Olímpio.

Oswaldo Pereira da Silva, construction manager, heard rumors that the building would be knocked down. He decided to try to come to an understanding with the padre, and suggested everyone wait until the bishop arrived. Josimo asked him if he'd stop the work and he said yes. Oswaldo sent word that work had been stopped and then heard that the building had been destroyed.

Sebastião Teodoro Filho (Donda), hotel keeper (and *pistoleiro*) said he saw Josimo, Lurdinha and Bia at the head of a band of one hundred armed men. He was unable to identify the weapons that Bia and Lurdinha were carrying. Josimo was armed with a machete. He had heard that there was an argument between the padre and the mayor, and that the people were planning to demolish the building. [Donda, brother to councilman Nenem, was murdered shortly before the assassination of Josimo.]

Davi Alves da Silva, shopkeeper, stated that the mayor had ordered work to begin, and that Josimo had advised him that it was church property. The padre had sent men to warn off the builders, and despite Oswaldo's attempts to come to an agreement, had supervised the destruction of the building. He stated that Josimo had used a megaphone, and that the Sisters had carried machine-guns. Afterwards, Josimo's group had left, shouting "Long Live Land Reform!"

The case hasn't come to anything yet, but for the inhabitants of Buriti, retribution was swift and brutal. The Federal Police were sent in to investigate, and on September 9th, they invaded the rural workers' union meeting and arrested thirteen people. One of the names on the list was that of Joâo Ananias; luckily for him, he wasn't present at the time. "I advised the boys not to have that meeting," he told me. "The Feds were hanging around, and I thought they were up to something. It was too easy. They found out what time the meeting would be, and they swooped down and picked everyone up. Some of them were freed, but the ones they were really mad at — Didi, Sebastião and Chico Sanfoneiro — were taken to Augustinópolis and given a real workover. They broke their ribs. It's against the law of course, but that didn't stop them. They were forced to implicate Josimo, which was what the police had been after all along.

"A couple of days later, the men were let go, dumped by the side of the road and told to start running. Those bastards were shooting at them as they ran. They'd been so badly beaten up, they could hardly move. Luckily, Josimo happened to be passing, and he picked them up and brought them home. We were all horrified when we heard what had happened. Quite a lot of people ran off into the forest to hide.

"Josimo took those three to Brasília to make a public protest. He put up notices all over the place telling what had happened. He told the press and made a lot of fuss about it, and that infuriated his enemies. I think that was when they started making serious plans to kill him. It was about then that one of the Sisters happened to overhear the mayor and one of his friends. They were laughing and joking. Then the mayor said, 'Come what may, we've got to get rid of the black priest.'"

Chapter Ten

Who is this Man?

As Josimo approached the last eighteen months of his life, he was living a life of intense conflict. He was in conflict with his fellow priests, who saw their job as administering the sacraments rather than getting involved in politics. He was in conflict with the authorities, who planned to develop the region into an area of cattle ranches, designed to service the export corridor of Greater Carajás. Sometimes he was in conflict with the very people he sought to help.

Josimo saw his work among the peasants primarily as a means of creating community. This was a difficult concept for people who had been repeatedly driven from their lands. It wasn't easily understood by those who live in isolation, those whose political experience was confined to accepting handouts from paternalistic politicians. It was hard for those on the very edge of survival to imagine that things could be different. Somehow they confused community with communism. They didn't know what communism was, but they feared and rejected it instinctively — the old-style church had taught them that communism was anti-Christian values, and the military government reinforced the notion that it was both evil and insidious.

Josimo did not behave like other priests. Many of his parishioners were unsure about how to approach him. He handled all this with compassion and understanding. He understood that profound changes took time. Here, he had one great advantage over his fellow priests. Being of peasant stock, he was accustomed to the deliberate rhythms of rural life, and if he felt frustrated at the slow pace of change he didn't show it. He saw his job as helping the people to analyze their situation, identify their common problems, and work out strategies for survival. Survival involved both individual and collective resistance, and this brought him back to the challenge of creating community.

He saw the option for liberation as the option for life itself. The old theology never seriously questioned the status quo, seeking only to alleviate the harshness of the people's existence through the practice of good works and charity. Good works were not enough for Josimo; he wanted to replace the old order with a society of justice and righteousness.

Many of his parishioners misunderstood and mistrusted him. His fellow priests withdrew their support, and sometimes actively denounced him. But his main enemies were the authorities and the large landowners, and they used every means at their disposal to fight him. On their side were ranged the police, the justice system, and the *pistoleiros*.

They did what they could to discredit his name. Rancher Belisário Rodrigues da Cunha of Santa Cruz, Buriti, described Josimo as "an outlaw, a lunatic and a madman." Town councilman José Lamarck called him "a stupid little priest." Adstonir Resende of the Ranchers' Association would remark after Josimo's death, "He was asking for it." Ronaldo Caiado of the Rural Democratic Union would point out that Josimo was no saint, and his colleague Salvador Farina would say that he who sows the wind reaps the whirlwind. Slowly and subtly, they would place the blame for his death on his own shoulders.

So, who is this man, Josimo? A man so loved, so hated. A divider of priests, a divider of people. A simple man, attractive yet not charismatic. Not a man who set himself up as a leader, despite the traditional prestige associated with his position. A man of peace, who daily faced the dilemma of defending his people against every sort of violence and humiliation. A man who lived his life with a brilliant intensity, a man who knew, perhaps, that his time was short. A man who loved to sing, to dance, to play football. A man who read voraciously, who loved films, who appreciated classical music. A man who was accessible to anyone, a man who would go anywhere, anytime, in answer to a need, a man who would give unstintingly of his time, his possessions, and his affection. Articulate and fearless, he was a man who recognized no limits.

Such a man was highly dangerous to his enemies. They responded by threatening him with death. He became in certain circles, a pariah — increasingly isolated, increasingly lonely. To assuage his loneliness, he turned more and more to the company of Sister Lurdinha.

A strong woman, dark, direct, heavy set, passionate, Lurdinha was from the distant state of Rio Grande do Sul on the borders of Uruguay. She had come to the Parrot's Beak out of compassion for its suffering people. Passionately interested in politics, she even left her order so that she could run for election on the ticket of the Workers' Party.

Both Josimo and Lurdinha were living through harsh times. The angel of death was very near. It was, perhaps, understandable that they should take refuge in each other's company. They made a good team, sparking one another off. Lurdinha's impulsiveness balanced Josimo's calm ways.

Some say they were lovers. Malicious tongues began to wag, and their transparent delight in each other's company provided ample ammunition for their enemies.

Who knew if Lurdinha, who left the church for politics, imagined that Josimo would leave the church for her? If for her, the outcome was logical and desirable, for Josimo, the struggle must have been intense. The joy of his heart would have been in clear contradiction to his priestly vows. It must have been the most difficult decision of his life. Must the fatherless boy, now a priest despised for his race and condemned for his politics, surrender his chance for companionship, for understanding, for love? Deep down, Josimo must have known where his chosen path would lead. Must he walk to his death alone?

And yet there was little time for Josimo to think this through. By the end of that year, 1984, the prospect of the first democratically elected government after twenty years of military dictatorship brought increased demands for land reform, and increased violence and repression on the part of the large landowners. It provided an extraordinary opportunity for Josimo to put his hopes and ideals into practice. Acting on Jesus' injunction to be the salt of the earth and the light of the world, Josimo flung himself once more into his work. He and his parishioners faced together that most basic of all moral questions: how shall we defend ourselves from violence? Do we have the right to kill in self defense?

Among Josimo's colleagues at the CPT, there was one who shared his love for poetry and his passion for justice. Pedro Tierra was luckier than Josimo. Instead of being murdered, he was jailed and tortured. I met him in the CPT head office where he sat surrounded by piles of documents on rural violence, and asked him about Josimo's views on the use of violence in self defense.

"First of all, we have no shred of evidence that Josimo ever counseled anyone to violence," he said firmly. "Having said that, I'm certain he must have taken part in discussions with the squatters planning self-defense – which was an extremely serious step for one in his position. The important thing, I think, was this. I believe that he took upon himself, understanding clearly what he was doing, the full dimensions of their lives. And those lives were inseparable from violence. So I wouldn't have been surprised if he had discussed it with them. The police and the authorities certainly thought so.

"They used to say there hadn't been any violence before Josimo arrived. Nonsense! Of course there was. There was the whole question of the guerrillas, for a start, and the brutal repression on the part of authorities like Major Curió — who went so far as to bomb the peasants. That was quite apart from the land conflicts. What Josimo did was to speak for the dispossessed. He gave them a voice, he gave them hope, and he showed them how to fight for their rights. So naturally, he was a terrible threat to the landowners.

"Josimo was an extraordinarily rich and complex personality, you know. Here's a man who goes around in old clothes and flip-flops, with a head full of Liberation Theology! He's so much bigger than his enemies. His horizons are much broader than theirs. His understanding is way beyond the society where he works, or the church he belongs to, or even the bishop to whom he owes allegiance.

"He's courageous and unconventional. He's endlessly patient. He never backs himself into corners, he's always ready to negotiate with his enemies. He understands the political realities, and particularly, the threats to the peasants posed by the Carajás project. He knows the government isn't in the least bit interested in a bunch of illiterate peasants living in the back of beyond. He can see that if they don't fight, they'll lose everything.

"So by taking up their case, he becomes a symbol for resistance and a focal point for hope. When people are evicted and beaten up, when their houses are burned down and their possessions stolen, what does Josimo do? He encourages them to go back onto the land, to resist at all costs, and never to despair. He is a free spirit, a strong tower, and to the ranchers he is insufferable.

"It's the old fight between free land and fenced land. Josimo was always fighting against fences, all kinds of fences. I talk about that in my poem for him. I see him always fighting.

> Against fences of fear.
> Fences of hatred.
> Fences round the land.
> Fences of hunger.
> Fences round living flesh.
> Fences round huge estates.

"By fighting against fences, Josimo poses a terrible threat to the large landowners. To them it is inconceivable that a black man should be a priest, or that a priest should be black. For generations they have been accustomed to dominating the laborers, and the fact that Josimo, a peasant himself, should speak for his people and denounce the landowners is unprecedented. He represents the unthinkable prospect of victory for the underdogs."

Chapter Eleven

The Enemy Musters

1985 was a year of hope for Brazil. Twenty years of military government had been succeeded by an infant democracy. The generals stepped aside, and even when president-elect Tancredo Neves was taken sick the day before assuming office, they made no move. The country held its breath while Tancredo agonized his way through his last illness and died. His place was taken by the vice-president, Jose Sarney, a large landowner and a favorite of the armed forces.

Sarney inherited a country that had been bankrupted by years of military excesses. It was essential he put his financial house in order, and since he needed support both from his foreign creditors and from the left wing of the Brazilian Democratic Movement Party who were pressuring him to sort out the land question, he announced an ambitious plan for land reform. With much fanfare, he stated his goals: within five years he would settle one million, three hundred thousand families on one hundred million acres.

The trades unions were delighted. The landowners were enraged. Their response was to found the Democratic Rural Union (UDR), an organization whose undeclared aim was to sabotage Sarney's plan. They were rich, they were smart and they were ruthless. They also figured it was time for a change of tactics.

Brazilian law gives a householder the right to defend his property — by force if necessary. For generations, the landowners had ruled in this manner, resolving any disputes by sending in their gunmen. They now began to arm themselves seriously, and to set up "security firms" whose business it was to supply armies of *pistoleiros*. Violence became big business. The landowners also began to choose their targets with greater care, concentrating on union leaders, lawyers, priests and church workers engaged in the land struggle. They drew up lists of troublemakers to be eliminated, and prominent on these lists was the name of Josimo.

There were a lot of people interested in silencing Josimo. The police, known to favor the ranchers, routinely described CPT staff as carrying arms, always referred to the small farmers as invaders, and never stopped to check the truth of the ranchers' claims to the land. They called Josimo a terrorist and made veiled death threats. One signed police report described a communal work effort on November 19th in Sumauma — João Custódio's village. It claimed that Josimo was at the head of a hundred men, all armed with rifles. It also stated that the village was defended by men in trenches.

Some of the soldiers who had served in the Araguaia guerrilla war turned into *pistoleiros*, and so did some of the military police. The lifestyle suited them and the money was good. One of these was former Lieutenant Trajano Bueno Bicalho, who went to work for Lourismar and Tomás Lobo on Fazenda Camarão. Lt. Trajano stated in a magazine interview, "We must get rid of this black priest and those foreign nuns who spend their time disturbing the peace." He was prepared to do the job himself, and was further quoted as saying, "What matters round here isn't what the sheriff says, isn't what the judge says, isn't what the president says; what matters round here is who's first on the draw."

The police didn't like Josimo, the *pistoleiros* didn't like him, and the judges didn't like him either. Most of them were in the pockets of the landowners anyway. Dr. Mauro Pires of Itaguatins was involved in the case of the telephone, and Judge Waltides Pereira dos Passes was in charge of the Canários/Palmério case. Neither of these two was known for dispensing impartial justice. The caliber of local judges can be assessed by the case of Judge João Batista de Castro Neto of Araguaina, who was said to have accepted the present of Fazenda Babassu, in Axixá, in exchange for overlooking the small matter of the murder of the former mayor, Joaquim Baltazar da Silva. The judge was in the habit of issuing summons without checking the full names of the summonsed, contenting himself with writing them out as "John Doe." He and his fellow judges also found a way round the disagreeable task of delivering eviction orders. By posting them on some tree in a distant town, they could ensure that the villagers would never see them, and would be unable to contest the eviction. Judge João Batista requested the presence of the military police on the basis that he had heard there was violence in the region and armed invaders menacing the ranchers' employees.

The ranchers didn't like Josimo either. The numerous family of Osmar Teodoro da Silva (Nenem) had sworn to get even with him after the death of Nenezão during the Augustinópolis demonstration. Guiomar Teodoro da Silva (known as Temtem) was later named in connection with Josimo's murder, although he was never detained. Joâo Teodoro da Silva, another brother who was questioned and released, admitted that there had been a meeting in his house to plan Josimo's death, but denied any responsibility. Sebastião Teodoro da Silva (Donda) was later to die in a shoot-out with the settlers, and his death was to be cited by the police as providing the motive for vengeance in the murder of Josimo — although once again, Josimo had no knowledge of the affair. Oswaldo Teodoro da Silva (Mundico) was also thought to be implicated. Nazaré Teodoro da Silva (Deca), the *pistoleiro* to whom I spoke, was living freely in Buriti six years after the murder, still openly practicing his trade. The only one who had been arrested was his brother-in-law, Vilson Nunes Cardoso, driver of the getaway car.

There were plenty more. Geraldo Vieira (Nó) was also implicated, together with his son, Adailson, and his neighbor, Sebastião Vigilato dos Santos. Adstonir Resende was the head of the local ranchers' association, and is considered to this day one of the chief enemies of the peasants. Joâo Japonês, owner of Fazenda Ouro Verde, blamed Josimo for the land invasion that resulted in the expropriation of part of his property, for which he was never indemnified. Crispim Batista, Fausto Rodrigues da Cunha, Esmeraldo Boni and Joaquim da Quinta Lima (the mayor of Araguaina) had also had problems with the peasants, and blamed them on Josimo. Rancher Hamilton José da Souza of Axixá accused Josimo of being directly responsible for at least 12 deaths. There were others who were implacably opposed to Josimo: Jair Rocha, Divino Prudente, Airton Jacob Barros, Joâo Borges, Dermival and Belisário Rodrigues da Cunha, Pedro Vernilo, Odilon Roriz, Geraldo Rosa da Cunha, Arlindo Gomes da Silva, Lourismar and Tomás Pereira Lobo... [These many names come from newspaper cuttings maintained by FASE (Federation of Socio-Economic Assistance) in Rio de Janeiro, whose file on the Josimo case is called "Dossier of a Death Foretold."]

In Latin America, there is a certain ritual that accompanies a death foretold. It starts with whispers, rumor, veiled hints. These are designed to isolate the victim from his support base. Hence the references to Josimo as communist, agitator, "not a proper priest." The presence of *pistoleiros*, who are regarded with fear and respect, sometimes even with admiration, is enough to make sure that everyone keeps out of the way. Rumors give way to a campaign of lies.

One journalist, Maria Apollo, published an article in a magazine called *Opinion* where she said the following:

> Padre Josimo seldom turns up in his parish for religious duties. When he does, he preaches violent solutions to the problems of the people who live there, as well as inciting them to armed land invasion, placing the people against their leaders. The village he visits most is the Centro dos Mulatos, which he has turned into a fortress. In order to get in there you have to know the password and be recognized by everyone, otherwise you risk death at the hands of armed *pistoleiros*.

As the news spread beyond the confines of the Parrot's Beak, an unattributed document was circulated in the presidential cabinet. It referred to Josimo as "adept at Liberation Theology, and the interpretation of the Holy Scriptures from a Marxist/Communist angle," described him as "responsible for a double homicide," and went on to state that he "organized the local Workers' Party, commanded all the land invasions in the region, and promoted collective disobedience to the laws of the land, teaching simple illiterate workers to disobey the law, and alleging that the only way to acquire squatters' rights was by land invasion, and then resistance — even to the extent of using firearms."

They called Josimo "a communist agitator of the worst type, who hides a blunderbuss beneath his robe." They said that the blood he loved was not the blood of Christ, but the blood of landowners. They warned that if urgent measures were not taken immediately, innocent blood would be shed, as it was by the worst dictatorships in Black Africa, and all because of the unscrupulousness of a handful of false prophets.

"IT'S THE BEGINNING OF THE END," they trumpeted. "WE ARE HEADING FOR CIVIL WAR IN THE COUNTRYSIDE."

They laughed at Josimo for being black. They said he was Lurdinha's lover. State prosecuting attorney Edna Búzio de Barros Rodrigues said that the Parrot's Beak used to be a peaceful area until the padre and some women "who claimed to be nuns" started disturbing the peace by telling people not to pay rent on their lands. She stated that Josimo and Lurdinha were responsible for the death of Palmério, and she considered them to be highly dangerous.

So dangerous that when Josimo and Lurdinha were arrested, they were refused *habeas corpus*. Brazilian law states that *habeas corpus* cannot be denied to those who have no criminal antecedents, but in this case, the judge reported that the fact that Josimo was a priest was not of itself a sufficiently good reason for granting his release. He further pointed out, quite improperly, that there were some priests who flee from the sacred mission of saving souls and teaching the love of God and one's neighbor, to take up revolvers and kill in cold blood, leaving orphaned children to grow into a generation of delinquents. Another judge in the Fourth Federal District of the state of Goiás was later to rule that Josimo was responsible for his own death.

With so many enemies sworn to get him, it seemed impossible that Josimo could survive for long. No one knows just how many attempts were made to kill him, but we know that in July, 1985, the *pistoleiro* Joâo Ester claimed to have been offered two million cruzeiros ($120,000) to kill Josimo. He said that the money was being raised by local ranchers.

In May, 1985, Josimo had his first lucky escape. He was going from São Sebastião to Sítio Novo for a meeting. He had lent his car to someone else, and was driving a borrowed VW Beetle. When he came to the second bridge after Augustinópolis, he found the road flooded for almost half a mile. A long line of cars was backed up on either side, waiting for the water to go down. One of Josimo's passengers tried to cross on foot, but was forced to turn back by the swirling water. A car drew up behind him, driven by Joâo Teodoro da Silva, sworn enemy to Josimo ever since the death of his brother, Nenezão. As the waters started to recede, the first trucks managed to make their way through. Josimo, always game for a challenge, headed his Beetle for the water and drove slowly and steadily through. Joâo Teodoro da Silva drove after him and his car stalled halfway across. Just as well for Josimo, since Joâo Teodoro had planned to kill him that day.

There were whispers and rumors, and plots and plans were hatched. Some of Josimo's parishioners were courageous enough to warn their priest. Much as they valued him, they begged him to leave without delay.

"Padre Josimo," they said on many occasions, "You must go away from here, otherwise they will kill you. Go away and never come back."

Chapter Twelve

A Death Foretold

"Of course, we never thought it would happen," said Edna, the catechist. She and I were sitting in the bare little office in the parish house in São Sebastião. "We knew all about the threats, but it seemed inconceivable that anyone would kill a priest.

"It was all very subtle. Just talk, to start with. Hearsay. People would say that Josimo was getting himself into a tight spot, and since it's such a small place, everyone got to hear. The *pistoleiros* used to drop a few hints here and there, and we used to have to warn Josimo when they were in town. There was a lot of gossip in Buriti, too. There were more ranchers there than here, and it wasn't just them, it was the shopkeepers, the dentist, everybody. You could feel their hostility. We used to laugh about it. 'We're not here to be loved,' we'd say to each other. 'We're here to work.'

"People had been used to Padre Stanislau, and when Josimo arrived, they could see at once that things were going to be different. He started talking about unions, communities and associations. They didn't think that was any of his business. Then there was the question of injustice. I think a lot of people before had just considered it a part of life — the will of God. When they lost a child, they'd say, 'It's God's will.' But Josimo would say, 'It's just the opposite. This child died because he was sick, he didn't have enough to eat, he didn't have any clean water to drink. He died because of poverty and exploitation. That's not God's will.' People understand that now, but they didn't then.

"It's like the land. Josimo used to say that the land is a gift of God to all men, not just to a few. He said everyone has the right to enough land to live on, because God put us all here to live, not to die. Of course, the ranchers didn't care for that sort of talk at all.

"We could see he was making enemies. We used to talk about it over supper. I used to say, 'Josimo, you know they're after you, don't you? People say they're going to kill you. Maybe you should leave for a while and let things cool down. You could even take the boat. That would be safer than driving. Everyone knows your car, and it wouldn't be difficult to ambush you on these roads.'

"He used to laugh at me. 'Oh Edna,' he'd say, 'You are a woman of little faith!' He'd say it jokingly, and when I thought about it afterwards, I didn't understand how he could joke about his death.

"It's hard to imagine now, but we got accustomed to it all. We got used to the threats. We never quite believed them. We did think, sometimes, that they might bring pressure on the bishop to move Josimo to another parish, but we never imagined... And at the time, we didn't know how often God had saved Josimo from death.

"For example, there was one time in 1985 when Josimo was coming back alone from Imperatriz. He'd planned to go one way, but ended up going another way. I can't remember why; I expect it was so he could give someone a ride home. He was always like that, he'd take the shirt off his back and give it to you if you needed it. We used to kid him about it; we never knew where our next penny was going to come from. No sooner would Josimo lay hands on his salary than he'd give it away. Dona Olinda and I would tease him about it and say, 'Now, Josimo, what in the world are we all going to eat?' But the funny thing was that we never went short. There was always enough, even if it was only rice and beans, or spaghetti. Anyway, on that day he came back a different way than usual, and we heard later that there'd been an ambush on the other road.

"You can't live if you're afraid for your life. I see that now. It's something you've got to come to terms with. Often the easiest thing is just to put it to the back of your mind. Josimo was good at that. He'd change the subject. 'Let's go play ball, Edna,' he'd say, and we'd run out in the yard like a bunch of kids. Or he'd pick up his guitar and say, 'How about a few songs tonight?' That always made us feel brave.

"There was so much to do, we didn't really have time to think about death. Perhaps it was just as well. Of course, as catechist, I stayed pretty much in the parish, keeping Dona Olinda company and helping out in the house. But Josimo was always on the move. You never knew where he'd be next. If the road was too bad, he'd roll up the legs of his pants and walk through the mud, just like anyone else.

"He used to travel farther afield too. He'd go to Goiânia and Brasília a lot, especially if he was lodging a complaint with the authorities. Sometimes he went to Rio; he belonged to an association of black priests there. He went several times to Carajás, because he wanted to see what they were up to. He used to say that the Carajás development project was the greatest threat to the land in these parts, because they had scheduled the Parrot's Beak as cattle raising land, and he could see the government wanted to get rid of the peasants. He'd say to them, 'You hang onto your land, because once you leave, you'll never have a chance to get back. And you'll end up working in the mines at Carajás.' He told us there was a plan to put in a huge dam at Itaguatins to generate power for the Carajás Export Corridor. I don't know how many people would have to move out. He used to say they'd expropriate the land anyway, even if they never did build the dam. By doing that, they'd get the people out, and they'd make sure they never got back in. He was interested in the whole Amazon region. He visited Santarem on the river Amazon, and he used to go to Belem too. That last year, he went to São Paulo and bought a sound system, because by that time all the people couldn't fit into the church, and half of them had to stand outside. It was a very small sound system, all he could afford, but the police later said he was using it to command armed men. Did you ever hear anything so ridiculous?

"If you look back on it now, you can see that he was a marked man, but somehow at the time we didn't realize it — probably because we didn't want to. There were rumors that the ranchers were up to something. They were selling chickens and goats at auction and people said it was to raise money to pay for a *pistoleiro*. People knew about it, but they didn't say, because they didn't want to get involved. They were afraid. You can't blame them.

"There was one woman who was always in and out of the house doing parish work. Her name was Doralina. I remember her scolding Josimo good and proper. 'Padre Josimo,' she said, 'It's not your job to be out and about. For one thing, it's too dangerous, and for another, your place is in the church.'

"Josimo smiled and said, 'Dona Doralina, people think the church is a place to pray in. What do you think?' She said, 'I don't really know.' So he said, 'The church isn't just a house. It's all the people coming together to talk about the things of God and the things of the world.' And she said, 'That's as may be, Padre Josimo, but I want you to stop all this.' He put his hand on her shoulder, and he said, 'Dona Doralina. There's no way I can stop all this now. But don't you worry about me. I'll be all right.'

"I used to ask him not to travel so much, especially towards the end. I'd say, 'Why don't you let me go with you? It's not safe you going alone; you never know what might happen.' He'd laugh and say, 'It's all very well, Edna, but people have got their work to do, they can't go around looking after me.'

"It wasn't until early in that year, 1986, that I started to think that, yes, perhaps they might try to kill him. I remember the weekend before the first attack. That Saturday, the military police arrested Didi, one of the hothead members of the union who was always getting into trouble, for illegal possession of weapons. After Mass, we went to São Sebastião to talk to the police. The sheriff wouldn't free Didi, but he promised to let him out next morning. Josimo suggested we hold an all-night vigil outside the police station, but everyone was tired, and in the end we went home to sleep. The moment we left, they hurried Didi over to Augustinópolis, and next morning we found the police station all locked up and Sergeant Mendes nowhere to be seen. We thought we'd better do something fast. Didi was one of those who'd been so badly beaten up after the Palmério affair — we were afraid what they might do to him this time. We sent for all his friends and took a hundred men over to talk to Zé Carneiro, the mayor, about it. He didn't like that at all, but we did get Didi out, and then we had a victory parade through São Sebastião and Buriti. That made the mayor even madder!

"Two days later, Zé Carneiro went to tell Josimo that he wanted to build the telephone exchange on the same place as before. Josimo was pretty smart about that. He said his hands were tied on account of the lawsuit. He suggested that Zé Carneiro withdraw it, then perhaps they could come to an agreement. At four o'clock that afternoon, Josimo left for Imperatriz. He hadn't got far when he discovered some problem with the steering on the car, so he had to stop in Augustinópolis for repairs. That delayed him and it was almost seven thirty when he left. He should never have been traveling after dark all by himself. The *pistoleiros* had been watching him all along. They knew. I think everyone knew."

In his eulogy for Josimo, Pedro Tierra wrote:

Everyone knew
The barbed wire fence of the huge estates knew,
The *pistoleiros*, hired agents of death,
the plain clothes police, the uniformed police,
        GETAT,
the gold miners, the drunks,
the good time girls,
the teachers, the nuns,
the children playing in the sandy streets, knew.

The men of the land, the settlers,
the dispossessed,
the women, raised in pain
and hope
knew.

The mayor, the judge, the chief of police,
the UDR,
the ranchers
knew.

The hands of the murderers
polished up their weapons.

The young shoots of the babassu palms
knew,
and bent their branches in a lament
telling the world of this death.

The birds, the clock telling the time,
counting the procession of the hours,
knew,
and didn't hold back;

The water of the rivers
never ceased to flow irrevocably towards
the hour of this death.
The stones on the road
knew
and were silent.
The wind
knew,
and proclaimed it
in its indecipherable moaning.

Your sandals
knew
and went on walking.

And I,
who was born for happiness,
and live to tell
the endless rosary
of deaths,
never wrote the poem
the sword of fury
which would cleave in two
the procession of the hours
and stop
the hour of your death.

You knew.
And you only smiled.
Like one who washes himself
to be ready, dressed
in cotton and transparency
for the hour of loneliness.

Chapter Thirteen

"I die for a just cause"

Tuesday, April 15th, 1986. It was seven thirty in the evening, and Josimo was behind schedule. He was trying to reach Imperatriz, and had been held up by a minor fault in the steering of the Toyota, forcing him to waste two hours on a repair in Augustinópolis. There was no escaping traveling by night, even though his friends had all warned him against doing so. It was a dark night and a lonely road, there were several single-lane bridges, and he was traveling through hostile territory.

Ten miles outside Augustinópolis, he noticed a car coming up behind him at high speed. It overtook him, leaving swirling clouds of dust. Josimo was driving slowly because he was not entirely happy about the Toyota's steering. Another car came up fast behind him with its lights on full beam, and Josimo hugged the right hand side of the road. The car caught him, slowed, dipped its lights, and drew abreast. Suddenly he heard what sounded like two stones violently hitting the bodywork. Seconds later, he saw a white Volkswagen Passat overtaking him, and, as in a dream, a hand pointing a revolver at him.

Josimo kept calm and kept driving, watching the other car as closely as he could. The assassin accelerated into the dust and darkness. Heart racing, Josimo waited to see if he would turn back, but he showed no signs of stopping. All alone, there was nothing Josimo could do. There wasn't a single house nearby. He had no choice but to turn back to Augustinópolis .

He drew up outside the police station and stopped to inspect the damage. Only then did he discover the full truth; five bullets had been fired at him, not two as he had first thought. One bullet hadn't perforated the body work; the other four were lodged inside the door.

The police station was shut. There was no one around. Josimo went to the newly-built barracks and found the chief of police. He begged him to get after the *pistoleiro* before he reached Axixá. The police chief told him that there were no radios in any of the police stations, and no way of getting in touch. Since he had no idea which way the attacker had gone, he was unable to give chase. The best he could do was to escort Josimo to wherever he wanted to go. Josimo had no alternative, and accepted an escort to a friend's house in Sampaio.

Next morning, Josimo returned to Augustinópolis to make a statement. The Toyota was taken to the workshop, the door dismantled, and the bullets removed. The police told Josimo they were from a 7.65 mm pistol, and that he owed his escape to the fact that it was fired at very close range. They went with him to the scene of the attack and took some pictures, and then continued to Axixá, since the crime was committed in that district. The police chief in Axixá told Josimo he would solve the case within thirty days.

But Josimo did not have thirty days left to live.

He continued under police escort to the ferry at Bela Vista and crossed to the town of Imperatriz. In his statement to the police, Josimo used some text he would deliver two days later to the Land Tribunal, an informal trial of land crimes held by the Brazilian Order of Lawyers in Belem. He wrote:

> It is clear to me that this attempt took place in the social context of the region and its land conflicts. The inhabitants of the Parrot's Beak, migrants from other states, are holed up on their lands, facing the violence of the land-grabbers. The ranchers, faced with the possibility that there may be a land distribution to the squatters, are arming themselves and trying to eliminate those people they believe to be the leaders of the peasants. What I suffered is the merciless, conclusive proof of their desire to prevent even the minimum implementation of land reform, since any attempt to enforce this plan will result in the loss of the enormous political and administrative power which they enjoy in this region. Since there were only two people in the car, the driver and the *pistoleiro*, it is likely that the car does not come from our area, but from another town. If this is the case, it reveals the existence of an extensive regional and even state-wide organization of large landowners opposed to Land Reform. We are talking about a force that is well organized to block any changes in land ownership, to

guarantee the election of its own candidates, and to undermine and destroy such political and organizational advances as the rural workers have been able to achieve during these last few months. From my point of view, this attack is the realization of innumerable death threats which I have been receiving for several months. These threats have come from ranchers and politicians, by word of mouth, in newspaper articles, in political speeches and meetings.

Despite all this I am determined to carry on the fight, trying to reconcile the need for peace with the Christian mission of creating a world of justice and righteousness, starting with the poor and oppressed. I pray for political understanding and strong faith, inspired by the resurrection of Jesus of Nazareth, the Christ.

Fighting words, and surely by then, Josimo must have realized that his enemies were in deadly earnest. He denounced them to the newspapers, the Council of Bishops, the Land Reform Agency and the Ministry of Justice, saying he was under considerable pressure from the right wing ranchers' union, the UDR. He pointed out that one of his chief enemies was João Japonês, who, he said, had personal motives for wanting to intimidate or eliminate him. Some days earlier, João Japonês' ranch had been invaded by evicted squatters, and in the resulting mêlée, several *pistoleiros* were killed. João Japonês and his fellow landowners were convinced that Josimo was the ringleader.

On Thursday, 17th April, Josimo's denunciation of the UDR was published in the daily paper, *Correio Brasiliense*, in Brasília. The UDR in its turn would later describe this article as "a rosary of accusations in the most elementary style of those who pretend to work on behalf of social justice, using the Bible to disguise their catechism of hatred. Their secret agenda incites peaceful laborers to take up arms, thereby increasing the suffering of those who already suffer unbearably. A man who presents himself as a priest of God affronts the basis of Christianity by disregarding the eighth commandment: Thou shalt not bear false witness."

That same day, Josimo testified at the Land Tribunal in Belem. Meanwhile, the Pastoral Land Commission sent a letter to Kurt Pessek at the Ministry of Justice Task Force Against Violence, saying they believed the *pistoleiros* would try again.

Back in Buriti, Lurdinha took Josimo to the barber to change his image.

Josimo's enemies intensified their efforts to discredit him. The UDR published a letter in the *Correio Brasiliense*, saying:

> There is no doubt that Padre Josimo has suffered a nasty shock with the recent so-called attempt on his life. The truth is that he is starting to reap the reward of the terrorism which has been growing for years in the north of Goiás, fertilized with sermons of great violence and irrigated with the blood of many innocent people.
>
> Ever since the time he fought with the guerrillas in Xambioá at the head of a band of thirty men armed with machine guns, ever since he headed the Workers' Party in Wanderlândia, leading invasions and teaching simple workers armed combat and disobedience to the laws, Padre Josimo has been the leader of various armed clashes between ranchers and troublemakers disguised as land invaders. At the beginning of April, Josimo led an invasion on Fazenda Ouro Verde, belonging to João Japonês, during the course of which several people died. [The UDR does not state that they were *pistoleiros*, who died in a shoot-out.]
>
> As the catalyst of such confusion, it is possible that one of his hundreds of victims may have responded with an attack on the padre, the preacher of the doctrine of hatred, violence and death.

Josimo had enemies closer to home as well. Some of his fellow priests and lay workers were strongly opposed to his political involvement and only too willing to add their voices to the rising tide of criticism. Scarcely was Josimo back from Belem, a seven hundred mile round trip, than he had to turn his attention to the First Diocesan Assembly in Tocantinópolis. He was coordinating the event, and more than a hundred people took part, including members of the clergy, nuns, pastoral and lay workers. They had a heavy schedule, and it was apparent from the start that there was considerable conflict between the traditionals and the progressives. This gave rise to heated discussions about the role of the Pastoral Land Commission. Josimo was called upon to give an account of his work, and to clarify the circumstances leading up to the assassination attempt. His reply, later written down, came to be known as his Spiritual Testimony. This is what he said:

Well, friends, I want you to understand that what has been happening is not the fruit of any ideology or theology, and has nothing to do with me personally. I believe the reasons for all this can be summarized in four points.

1. That God called me with the gift of priestly vocation and I responded.

2. That bishop Dom Cornélio ordained me.

3. That I was supported in my studies by the people of Xambioá and their padre, Joâo Caprioli.

4. That I committed myself to this type of pastoral work, which, through the strength of the Gospel, led me to work for the poor, the oppressed and those who suffer injustice.

As Jesus said, 'The disciple is not greater than his master. If they persecute Me, they will persecute you also.'

I have to accept this responsibility. I am engaged in the struggle for the poor defenseless workers, held fast in the clutches of the large landowners. If I do not speak for them, who will defend them? Who will fight for them?

I, at least, have nothing to lose. I have no wife, no children, nor any riches. No one will weep for me. My only regret is on account of my mother who has no one but me. She has no family and no money. But you will stay here and take care of her.

Even fear will not hold me back. It is time to stand up and be counted. I die for a just cause.

I want you to understand this; everything that is happening is the logical consequence of my work in defense of the poor, and in favor of the Gospel which led me to take on this commitment to the end. My life is worth nothing compared to the deaths of countless laborers who have been violently thrown out of their lands, leaving women and children abandoned, without love, without food and without shelter.

"It is time to stand up and be counted," Josimo said. "I die for a just cause."

But he couldn't know it would be so soon.

Chapter Fourteen

Living in the Shadow of Death

Everyone noticed how Josimo changed after the first attempt on his life. He became much quieter, much more thoughtful. Those who lived closest to him said he used to lock himself in his room for hours on end, praying. His nerves were strung taut.

One day, he dropped by the union in Sítio Novo. He told people there about the attempt on his life. They did their best to dissuade him from traveling alone. "I have to go," he repeated, obstinately. "They're not going to kill me."

He visited one of the small communities with Joâo Custódio, and chose that moment to talk about death. "Has it occurred to you, Joâo," he said, "that we might get killed in this work? After all, Christ was killed. We all have to die one day. I think perhaps I shall die soon."

"What foolish talk is this?" answered Joâo Custódio roundly.

"Can't you see it, Joâo? All the threats, the ranchers, the *pistoleiros*?"

"Come on," retorted Joâo. "This is silly talk."

But Josimo wasn't listening. He turned to Joâo. "If I die in this fight, will you give up?"

"I never forgot that," said Joâo, later. "It made me think of Peter denying Christ."

The last time the nuns saw him was the first weekend in May.

"It was his weekend to come to Mulatos," Mada told me. "By that stage, we were convinced they'd try to kill him, but somehow, nonetheless, we thought there'd be time for him to get out. We never expected it so soon. I remember he came to Mulatos and on Sunday we went down to Esperantina. Bia must have had some sort of a hunch because she wouldn't let Josimo drive the Toyota.

"'You're much too obvious a target,' she told him. 'I'll drive and you can sit in the back.' We went to Esperantina and we never saw anything unusual. Afterwards, we heard there'd been a strange car with two men in it hanging round all weekend. We reckon it must have been the *pistoleiros*. Esperantina was such a little place in those days that people noticed that sort of thing. But they didn't tell us at the time."

Dom Aloísio heard about the assassination attempt when he was at the conference of the Brazilian Council of Bishops in São Paulo state. The Council issued a letter of protest and sent it to the President of the Republic, with copies to everyone they could think of. Dom Aloísio rounded up the bishops of the Central West region and took them down to Brasília to talk to President Sarney and the Minister of Justice, Paulo Brossard. They pointed out that Josimo's life was in grave danger, and asked for protection. No steps were taken.

"Josimo understood the danger all right," Dom Aloísio told me. "He was very frightened. We had already started to take precautions. We told him not to travel alone, not to go out at night. We told him there was a strong chance that they'd try again. I knew how serious the situation was, but I didn't expect anything to happen so soon. I was going to send him south for a few weeks until things cooled off -- to the Benedictines in São Paulo.

"I started to get very anxious after the first attack. By that time, they'd already tried once, but we never heard about it until the *pistoleiro* Geraldo told us. He said the men who had hired him were very angry with him, swore at him, and told him he was an idiot to let the padre drive past under his nose. They raised the price after that first time so that Geraldo would try again. We never told Josimo not to worry, we never said it was all talk. We warned him to be very very careful. It was a classic death foretold."

Pedro Luis Dalcero, the young CPT lawyer, spoke to Josimo about it two days before the end. "Josimo was afraid," he said to me. "We all were. No one wants to die. I spent two hours talking to him about it, discussing whether he should leave. The bishop was pressuring him to go, and he liked the idea of going away to study. He wanted to do a Bible course in Paris, only he couldn't leave the country while they still had those lawsuits against him: the telephone and the murder of rancher Palmério. I think, myself, that Josimo was a bit confused. I could feel that when we were talking.

It was a terrible dilemma for him, and he felt it would be wrong to run away. I don't know if he changed his mind later."

Of all Josimo's friends, Lurdinha was the one who felt it most.

"I was in Imperatriz the day of the first attack," she said. "I was due to meet Josimo there and he didn't show up. I had lots to do and couldn't wait. Next day I heard about it, and since he had to go to Belem, I offered to go with him. I felt I had to be with him.

"He knew he was going to die. He became much quieter, more thoughtful. He used to sit in the house and say, 'Lurdinha, what will you do after I die? I worry for my mother, and for you. A lot of people will cry for me, but it'll be hardest on you two. You'll never forget me, even if the others do.'

"He kept talking about his death. Singing funeral songs. I said to him, 'Josimo, for Heaven's sake, stop all this.' We had gone to see some of the old women who sing songs at wakes. There was one song Josimo particularly liked. It was all about the angels coming to carry the souls of the dead to paradise. He recorded that song, and he used to sing it over and over. He said 'When I die, I want you to sing that song at my funeral.' He must have had a premonition. I think what they called his spiritual testimony was the result of all that thinking.

"One day at the very beginning of May, I dropped into the CPT office in Imperatriz and found Josimo sitting there all by himself with the door open. I shouted at him, 'What in the world are you doing?' He told me Domingos was working there with him and had just left that very minute. I shut the doors. There were two offices, and Josimo was in the outer one, right by the door. It was a hot day, and I went into the bathroom to take a shower. When I was in the shower, I heard someone trying to open the office door. I said, 'Who's there?' but there was no reply. All of a sudden, I knew what it was: someone was after Josimo. I bundled Josimo into the bathroom and told him to lock himself in. I called and called, trying to find out who it was, but they didn't say a word, just kept on trying to force the door. I got so panicky that I ran into the back room. There's a window there that looks over the garden of the bishop's house, and I thought I'd shout for help. Then I felt a bit silly, so I went back to check the outer door one more time. I didn't want to make a fuss about nothing— my nerves were all on edge. I tiptoed in and knelt down on the floor to see if I could see any feet outside. There was nothing there. I opened the door and couldn't see anyone, so I ran down into the street to ask if anyone had seen anything, but they all said no. Afterwards I wondered if they had seen something and were afraid to talk.

"Domingos and I heard that there were *pistoleiros* staying in the hotel in Augustinópolis, and we went there to check it out. Sure enough, Geraldo had been there the time of the first attack, but he'd left immediately afterwards. No one was prepared to talk either, much less testify in court.

"People who warned us were always terrified they'd be found out. They begged us not to tell anyone what they had said. The day they told us about the meeting in Augustinópolis to plan Josimo's death was the day he got really scared. He said to me, 'Do you think it's true?' And I said, 'Yes. I think it's time you left.' We discussed it and decided he must leave that very week.

"We kept talking to Josimo about leaving, doing everything we could to persuade him. It wasn't as if he was a martyr. He was always perfectly amenable to reason. We did manage to persuade him once. He went away on a Monday, but he was back on the Wednesday. 'It's no good,' he told us. 'I can't run out on these people. After all, they have no place to run.'

"The last time we went to Imperatriz to get the pictures of the Toyota with the bullet holes, we were stopped by two laborers at a place called Dez. They were really scared. They called Josimo over to a place in the square where no one could overhear, and they told him he must leave immediately. They said, 'You don't know what danger you're in. Don't tell anyone we told you, and never come here again. Go away today and don't come back because Deca's family wants to kill you this very week. Go away because you'll be dead if you stay. We want you alive, not dead. Don't tell anyone we told you.'

"Another time we were in the workshop in Augustinópolis. Josimo was having the body work on the Toyota fixed. It was after the first attack. We were inside, and Deca's son arrived. He didn't see us, and spent a long time examining the car, checking the tires, the bodywork, everything.

"I was with Josimo all that last week. He was in a bad state. We were having a schools meeting and we had to visit all the communities telling them about it. Josimo wouldn't even get out of the car. He used to send me in to talk to them. We went to the photographers to get the pictures of the Toyota, and he sent me to pick them up. He didn't even get out of the car to pay his bills. He was frightened. When we went to the CPT in Imperatriz, I used to run in first to open the door so he could get in, and I'd go back to lock the car. He was really nervy. Once a stone hit the windshield and he was scared to death. I said, 'Don't worry, Josimo, it's only a stone, it's not a bullet.'

"It was on the Wednesday that we heard they'd murdered Donda. He was another one of Nenem's brothers, and just as bad as the rest of them. He was working on Pedro Vilarino's place, and he was in charge of contracting out the sharecropping. He demanded such a monstrous share of the harvest that he got into a fight with the sharecroppers and ended up getting himself shot. They must have been pretty mad at him, because they wouldn't allow anyone in to collect his body. Apparently Donda had killed somebody not long before and wouldn't let the relatives take the body — said it could rot right there on the ground. So that's just what they said about his body. They sent a message to say Nenem couldn't take it till the dogs had eaten it. Nenem blamed it all on Josimo, and sent the police round to talk to him. Josimo didn't know anything about it. It wasn't even in his parish.

"When we heard about it, I said to Josimo, 'They'll arrest us again.' And he looked at me very straight and said, 'No, Lurdinha, this time they'll try to kill us.'"

Over on Fazenda Novo Mundo, attempts to retrieve the body of Donda were met with gunfire. Some said the squatters just didn't want the police around. The police came to enlist Josimo's assistance in negotiating with the squatters, but Josimo pointed out that he knew no more about it than they did. People were saying the Federal Police had been called in.

"It was on the Friday that the rumors started," said Lurdinha. "Everyone said things were very dangerous for Josimo. They blamed him for Donda's death, even though he had nothing to do with it. It wasn't even in his parish. Josimo came here on Friday morning, and by that stage the place was buzzing. The people in Vila União were very frightened; a lot of them had gone to hide in the forest.

They had nothing to do with Donda's death, but they expected trouble anyway.

"We could see how dangerous it was for Josimo. We stopped in at Hugo's house — he lives right next to Deca. Hugo's wife is a teacher and we were going to have a school meeting, so that gave us an excuse to call on her. Hugo came in while we were talking and told us there was a meeting going on at Deca's place. Zé Carneiro was there, and a lot of the ranchers. They were discussing how they were going to rescue Donda's body. They were saying it was all Josimo's fault. They said that police reinforcements were coming next day from Araguatins.

"Domingos and I could see all the cars in front of Deca's house, and we didn't like the look of it at all. We rushed home and told Josimo, and that really got to him. We sat down to discuss what was best. We wanted him to spend the night in Buriti, but he said he had too much work, and in the end he went back to São Sebastião.

"Later that evening, I started hearing rumors. People told me the ranchers were planning to kill Josimo and this time they wouldn't miss. At ten o'clock, old Dona Maria came running to the house saying they were going to kill Josimo the next day. She looked at me with her eyes full of tears and said, 'Tomorrow our padre is going to die. You must do something.' She used to foresee things. I think she had the second sight. She'd hardly walked out the door when Hermílio came running up and said, 'Lurdinha! I've just heard the police are coming tomorrow to arrest Josimo. They're going to send a helicopter to collect Donda's body, and then they are going to attack Buriti. Josimo can't stay around here.'

"We decided that Josimo should get out of São Sebastião before sunrise. We knew he was being watched, but we reckoned he could get out ahead of them. So I sat down and wrote him a note. I told him to leave immediately, not to delay for a second."

Over at Deca's place, the ranchers were putting the final touches to their plan. In Imperatriz, Geraldo the *pistoleiro* was having a night on the town, popping pills and drinking a great deal too much beer. In São Sebastião, Olinda and Edna were frying potato chips in the kitchen and Josimo was joking that he would live to be eighty -- if they didn't get him at thirty-three. But he didn't fool

Edna; she knew how tense and preoccupied he'd been these last days.

"Don't worry, Josimo," she whispered. "You'll be all right."

Josimo turned to her with a half smile. "Well, Edna," he said in a low voice. "If I die, do you think they'll call me a martyr?"

◆ **Chapter Fifteen** ◆

And Death the Journey's End

Saturday, May 10th, 1986, the day before Mother's Day, dawned a beautiful day in São Sebastião. Hermílio arrived on his bicycle and delivered a message from Lurdinha, urging Josimo to leave town. Josimo had to drop by the school to check on the arrangements for Mother's Day. Somebody wanted to borrow the Toyota for a Workers' Party procession. "I'm taking it in to Imperatriz today," Josimo said. "There are a couple of things need fixing."

Somebody else delivered a phone message that Dom Aloísio wanted Josimo to stop by and see him in Tocantinópolis. Josimo knew exactly why. The bishop wanted him out before anything happened.

Domingos slung his bag into the back of the Toyota. "It's OK," Josimo grinned. "I'd rather you took a message for me to the Sisters in Mulatos. I won't be traveling alone. I'm certain to find passengers at this time of day."

Domingos frowned as he removed his bag. He didn't feel happy about letting Josimo go alone. Before he could protest, Josimo swept up his things, clapped a straw hat on his head, and jumped into the Toyota. "See you next week, Mother," he said.

Giving her a quick hug, he was off.

Saturday, May 10th, dawned a beautiful day in Imperatriz, too. Perpétua was finishing up some oddments in the CPT office. A glamorous thirty year old with long brown wavy hair, she spoke emotionally about the day that marked her life.

"The tenth of May, that fatal day. I can't forget it. It was a very hot day, lots of sun — the day before Mother's Day, a beautiful day, not a day for terrible things to happen.

"We were buying presents for Mother's Day. Amparo and I were in the office. I had some bits and pieces of work to clear up, and Amparo was keeping me company. All of a sudden, we heard two shots. We joked about them. I said, 'Must be a firework,

Amparo,' since the June festival was coming up. She said, 'No, Perpétua, that's not a firework, it's a bullet.' She was on the phone at the time, and the person on the other end heard it, too. That gave me a fright. We dropped everything and ran out. Amparo said, 'Downstairs,' and I ran down. When I got downstairs, I saw a whole lot of people looking up into our building. So I thought — upstairs.

"I ran back up, and suddenly I saw Josimo. He was clutching his chest, and I could see blood on his shirt. I grabbed his arm, supporting him. He was swaying on his feet — I didn't think I could hold him up. I yelled for Amparo. We helped him down the stairs, then some men came up and carried him. Josimo couldn't speak. My chief concern was to get him to the hospital, quick. I said to Amparo, 'You take him, and I'll shut up the office.' We work with a lot of confidential matters, and I didn't want to leave the office open. It was an extraordinary moment of lucidity in the midst of such tragedy.

"I closed the office, then ran downstairs again. I had blood all over my hands. Then I saw them in a corner -- the two cartridges. I put them in my bag and glanced at my watch. It was 12:10. I ran next door to tell the bishop, Dom Alcimar. He was just coming back from lunch.

"I didn't want to upset him, but somehow the words didn't come out right. I started to say, 'They've killed...' and I couldn't get the name out. The bishop shouted, 'Who was it? Who was it?' and I said 'Oh,' and he said, 'Ah... Josimo? They've killed Josimo.' I couldn't speak. I just showed him the cartridges.

"They sat me down in one of the offices because they thought I was all upset. But I couldn't possibly stay there. I had to find Amparo and see what was going on. I waited until they'd all gone off somewhere, and then I made a break for it.

"I didn't know which hospital to look in. I checked out three, and then I found Amparo in São Marcos. She'd gone to the nearest one. Today, looking at things more calmly, I can see that another hospital might have been better. São Marcos isn't one of the best, but it was the closest. When I got there, I asked where Amparo was, and they said, 'In the pre-op room.' I ran in there, and the first thing I saw was Josimo. They were preparing him for surgery, shaving him. He was very pale, cold and sweating. He'd obviously lost a lost of blood. I took his hand, and I said, 'Josimo! How are you?' and he just gave me the thumbs up. The nurse said he couldn't talk — doctor's orders. So I said, 'Josimo, everything is going to be all right,' and he made a thumbs up.

"For the rest of my life, I'll never forget that gesture. A man who'd been all shot up, still steadying others at a time like that. He was always good at that sort of thing. His face was very calm, very peaceful. Not in pain or despair. Of course, I wanted to find out what had happened. He must have seen the assassin, and he might have had an idea who it was. But he couldn't talk. Afterwards, I asked Amparo if he'd said anything, and she said he'd asked the driver to go faster because he didn't think he'd make it. That was all he said. After he'd gone into surgery, I spoke to the nurse to find out if he'd said anything else. 'He did say one thing,' she told me. 'He said, 'This time I'm not going to get away with it.'

"If we'd taken him to another hospital... but I believe we all have our days numbered. It's so tempting to make excuses. If things had been different, if we'd gone elsewhere... but I don't know. The bullet entered his kidney and damaged all his insides. I don't see how he could have survived. But it's true, the hospital could have been better. They weren't very efficient. It was lunch time, and the anesthetist took a long time to arrive."

"Was there any suspicion of undue negligence?" I asked. "I shouldn't think medical care in Imperatriz is very good even now?"

"Too right, it's not," said Perpétua. "It's very poor. Those who can afford it go to Teresina for treatment."

I pursued the question. "Could you prove any negligence?"

"Well, the doctors have their own Mafia, of course. And the anesthetist was dreadfully slow in coming, so that held things up for forty minutes or so. But I couldn't say if they did it on purpose. One could speculate, perhaps... but there's no proof."

"After I'd got him admitted into hospital, I rushed to the phone," Amparo took up the story. "I called Dom Aloísio collect. I gave Josimo's name. I told him just what had happened, and asked him to come right away. He asked me how Josimo was, and I said to him, 'Honestly, I don't know if he'll live or not. I don't want to frighten you, but I have to tell you the truth.' Dom Aloísio said he was leaving directly.

"Then Perpétua arrived, and I asked her to stay while I made a few calls. I called Dona Olinda, but she was out and I couldn't leave a message for her. The news would have spread like wildfire, and Josimo's enemies would have been delighted. So then Perpétua and I went down to the police station."

"They were terrible to us," put in Perpétua. "I think they thought we were making the whole thing up. I had to show them the bullets before they'd believe us. I don't know how they could think it was a joke — me with blood on my clothes. I left the cartridges with them to prove our story."

"The police commissioner said someone had already notified them by phone, and it wasn't necessary to register again," added Amparo. We'd passed by the shop where the *pistoleiro* had parked his car, and we questioned the girl there about it. She didn't want to say anything, she was scared. We talked to the manager and told him it was crucial for us to have the number and a description of the car, and he persuaded the girl to tell us. So we had all this information when we went to the police. The commissioner said he didn't need all that. I said, 'I want to make a statement. It's my right. I want to make a statement and I want to sign it.' He said, 'That won't be necessary,' so we stormed out. By that time, the press were on our heels. We went back to the phone; we called everyone we could think of. We called the hospital to see how Josimo was getting on. I called, and the doctor answered. I asked how the surgery went, and he said, 'So-so.'

"'What do you mean?' I shouted, and he said, 'He didn't make it.'

Chapter Sixteen

May 10th, 1986

People always remember very clearly where they were at a moment of tragedy. "I was a good half mile away when I heard about Josimo," Carlinhos told me. "I ran without stopping all the way to the hospital. I think I sensed it was the end."

Carlinhos was a young agronomist who had recently arrived to join the CPT team. His job was to help the settlers improve their techniques so that they could make something of their hard-won lands.

"I was completely horrified," he continued, his face clouding. "I was visiting a friend. Someone told me that a black padre had been killed, and I knew at once. I said 'It's Josimo!'

"I ran straight to the hospital. I got there about twenty minutes after Josimo had been shot. They wouldn't let me see him at first, so I took the key of the Toyota from his bag and ran back to the CPT office. I wanted to shut it up and collect the car. Then I ran to find a telephone. I was desperate to tell Josimo's mother, Dona Olinda. I knew her quite well, and she had always treated me kindly. I'd recently arrived from the south and she was the first person to welcome me; she was like a mother to me. I had to let her know. But she wasn't there when I called. So I called the CPT head office in Goiânia, and the bishop in Tocantinópolis, and then I ran back to see how Josimo was getting on.

"After I went out to make those calls, I must have been back in ten minutes at the most. I went charging back and that time they did let me in. Josimo was covered in a white sheet, and there was blood all over the floor. He was breathing very slowly, and I didn't like the look of him at all. I rushed over to him, and I called out, 'Josimo!' He opened his eyes and closed them again. He looked like he wanted to talk, but the nurse said he mustn't. If he'd spoken, it would have forced him to breathe harder and he would have died sooner.

"When I saw him, he was still breathing. I thought he was bad, but I didn't know he was dying. I didn't know how much damage the bullet had done. I told people he was bad because when I called, he didn't answer.

"It took the doctor a long time to show up. The hospital staff couldn't find the damn doctor, can you believe it? It was Saturday, it was lunch time. I was pleading with them to do something, but what could I do? I was new to the area, I didn't know the doctors, I didn't know the system, and I didn't know a soul in Imperatriz. The doctor didn't show up till almost two o'clock. By that time, they were getting Josimo ready for the operating theater, and they kicked me out. I waited outside for an hour, pacing up and down. There were four or five other people there as well. I didn't know any of them. They wouldn't let us in.

"I should have gone in there with him, but I didn't know any better. If it had been today, I'd have done it differently. But it's no good crying about it, because it's all over. That's what's so awful about it. It's all over.

"Then the doctor came out and said Josimo was dead. He asked if there were any family members present, and before I could say anything, three men barged into the room. I didn't know who they were, and it wasn't until afterwards that I realized what was going on. They'd gone in to check that he was dead. It's all part of a *pistoleiro's* job.

"I was devastated. I just sat down and wept. And then one of the nurses came up to me, and said, 'Was that black man a friend of yours?'

"And I said, 'Yes, he was.'

"So she said, 'Well, he was quite something, that one. I was on admissions when he came in. In he comes, on his feet, dripping blood all over the place, and walks up to me cool as a cucumber and asks the way to surgery.

"'Upstairs,' says I, and he just nods and starts walking.

"'Hey!' I says, 'Just a minute! There's a trolley here.'

"'That's OK,' says he, 'I don't need it.'

"'Yes, you do,' I tell him, 'You get up there.'

"And he gets up on the trolley, lies down and closes his eyes. What an extraordinary thing. I've never seen anything like it. He was all shot to bits. Yet he came in on his feet. Most people in that state come in carried by others, but not this one. He was tough. An iron constitution.'

"So Josimo climbed up on that trolley and lay down and closed his eyes, and that's what killed him. He drowned in his own blood. They should have made him sit upright.

"After he died, I took his things — his clothes, his sandals, and his shirt. I put them in a bag, all bloody. I kept them. I have them still.

"He must have run up that second flight of stairs after Geraldo shot him. Ran up, turned left, and by the time Perpétua and Amparo came out, he'd already gone round the corner. That's why they didn't see him. He was carrying a bag of clothes and a huge pile of books and files. He managed to unlock the office door, and then he dumped them down. Half of them fell on the floor. I could tell that nobody had been in there since then, because he'd left some money on the table and it hadn't been taken. When I got there, the door was ajar and the key was still in it. I thought I'd better leave everything as it was.

"I went back later to get some decent clothes for him, but he didn't have any. He had nothing but old clothes in his bag, all crumpled. It looked like he'd packed in a hurry. And he must have just slung his stuff through the door. It was all he could manage. He was so badly hurt: kidneys, liver, lungs, all perforated. Intestines too."

"He never told anyone who it was?" I asked gently.

"No," sighed Carlinhos. "When I saw Amparo at the hospital, I asked if he had said anything, and she told me he urged the driver to hurry because he wasn't feeling good. He said he couldn't die. But he didn't talk to me. He couldn't speak, he just looked at me. If I'd been more experienced I'd have lifted him up so he could talk. I never thought he was going to die."

Carlinhos' brother, Domingos, had gone that day with Edna and Dona Olinda to visit the nuns in Mulatos. He was to give them a message from Josimo asking them to meet him next day in Tocantinópolis. Mada was horrified when she heard that Josimo had gone to Imperatriz alone.

"I didn't even say hello!" she recalled. "I said, 'Where's Josimo?'

"'Gone to Imperatriz,' they said.

"I yelled at Domingos. 'You let him go alone? Whatever were you thinking of? He should never have gone on his own.'"

"Domingos hung his head at that," Mada said. "But by that time it had already happened."

"It wasn't Domingos' fault," Edna told me hotly. "He was all set to go with Josimo. He had his bag in the car and all. It was Josimo who said he didn't need anyone with him, and asked if he'd go leave a message with the Sisters.

"But Mada was obviously worried stiff, and that got us worried too. So we didn't stay long. Not more than half an hour. They were having a Bible study, and we didn't even stay for lunch.

"We were on the way back when we saw a car coming. The driver flagged us down, and then we saw that it was Didi. He'd recently been in jail, and my first thought was that he'd gotten himself into trouble again. We half thought of not stopping because we didn't recognize the man he was with, and wondered if it might be a *pistoleiro*. But Didi put out his hand. As we got out, we could tell by his face that something terrible had happened. He said, 'I came to tell you that Josimo has been shot.'

"Olinda gave such a start that she hit her head on the roof. And then she went into a kind of faint. We all tried to console her, saying that he wasn't going to die. What else could we say? But I think I knew even then."

"I couldn't concentrate on the Bible study after I heard that Josimo had gone off alone," said Mada. "So we decided to finish up early, and we were almost through when another car arrived. It was João Ananias and Didi. João jumped out of the car and came running up. He said, 'They've shot the man.'

"It's not a way of speaking I care for. Referring to people as 'the man' or 'the woman.' But I knew at once that it was Josimo. We didn't know if they'd killed him. We kept praying he'd live."

Domingos took up the tale. "Someone called through from Imperatriz to say that Josimo was dead, and the ranchers started celebrating right away. They threw a party in Augustinópolis. When the word got to São Sebastião, the entire community went to the parish house. When we got there, I went in and collected Olinda's clothes, put them in the car, and drove straight to the turnoff to wait for the Sisters.

"You can imagine how I felt. Then, all of a sudden, a car drives up and there's the mayor, Zé Carneiro. 'Oh Domingos,' he says to me. 'I've just heard the dreadful news. Would you like me to escort you to Imperatriz? It might be safer if I went with you.'

"'Go with you?' say I. 'Whatever for? You've already done what you set out to do.'

"I knew, you see, that he'd been gunning for Josimo for a long time. The night before, I happened to be in the telephone exchange in São Sebastião when Zé Carneiro arrived back from Goiânia and stopped by to make a call before even going to his house. While he was there, they told him of the death of Donda. Zé Carneiro lived right by the telephone cabin in the house on the corner. Here's this man, just traveled the best part of a thousand miles, and instead of going home to relax, he dropped off his bag and set out immediately for Buriti. And you know what he did in Buriti, don't you? He took part in that meeting at Deca's house. He planned the murder of my best friend, and then had the gall to offer himself as my bodyguard the very same day." Domingos flushed angrily at the memory. "I turned him down flat, and then he swanned over to Dona Olinda and started sympathizing with her — with the blood of her son on his hands."

João Ananias had gone with Didi to take the news to Dona Olinda and the Sisters.

"What happened in Buriti when the news came through?" I asked him.

"It made a lot of people happy," said João matter-of-factly. "One of the girls in the telephone exchange was so delighted that she slammed down her stool hard enough to break it."

I turned to Mara. "What did you think?"

"*Avé Maria!*" said Mara. "What a shock it was. When we went to the telephone cabin, that same woman who broke the chair saw Didi and called him over to tell him she had heard that Josimo was dead. I ran up to her and said, 'How do you know, Maria?' and she told me there'd been a call from Imperatriz."

"I told Mara we'd better get moving," put in João. "So we found a car, and we set off for Mulatos to tell Olinda. We met them on the road. I got out and went over. I was so agitated I could hardly speak. I told her straight. I could have done it better but I couldn't find the words, I was in such a state. I said, 'Something terrible has happened. They've killed Josimo.'

"Domingos said to me, 'You'd better go to Mulatos and tell the Sisters.' After that we came back to Buriti and hired a truck to go to the wake at Tocantinópolis. It was on the way there that Mara nearly got killed."

"How ever did that happen?" I asked Mara.

"We'd stopped at the gas station in Augustinópolis," said Mara. "I was sitting by the door of the cabin when Nenem drove past in a little car. He'd obviously been drinking, and he was shooting in the air. The bullet missed my head by inches.

"We went on to Tocantinópolis, and I got out of the truck trembling like a leaf. My God, what a night that was. We slept right there in the truck.

"It was the bishop's idea to have the funeral in Tocantinópolis. He thought there might have been trouble if we'd had it here. At first, I thought he meant trouble from Josimo's supporters, but he told me later he was afraid of what the ranchers might do. Tempers were running high, so it's true something might have happened. Someone might even have been killed."

"Do you think the bishop was right?" I asked.

"Well, honestly, I suppose he was," said Mara. "On the one hand. But on the other... Josimo was our padre, he deserved to have his funeral here where he lived and worked. He always used to say to us, 'You are my family,' and because it was in Tocantinópolis, we couldn't all go.

"You can imagine how we felt. We were all so angry. Everyone: young, old, the children, even the men. We weren't just weeping tears of sorrow. They were tears of rage. Tears demanding revenge. To this day, the men who organized Josimo's death are free. They've never even been arrested. And what can we do? We don't have the means to fight them. They have the guns, and we don't. People say the countryside is ready to explode. But how can we fight without guns?

"But we could still have taken our revenge. The only reason we didn't was because of the padres. They didn't let us. They should have let us do what we wanted. Zé Carneiro was behind Josimo's death. Everyone knew that. Yet there he was at the funeral, and he actually got up and spoke! Can you imagine? We were furious. We'd have strung him up there and then if the padres hadn't been so lily-livered.

"And what would Josimo have thought of that?" I asked. "Surely he was opposed to violence?"

"Yes he was," answered Mara. "He never once counseled us to react violently. We needed to let off steam, but he wouldn't have liked it. You're right. He didn't want bloodshed. But one day, we'll have our revenge."

"Tell me about the funeral service," I said.

"I think it was the worst day of my life," said Mara. "It's not as if I don't know what death is about. I've lost both my parents, and one of my babies. But somehow this was the greatest loss of all. Everyone felt it. We were all desolated. We felt it was all over.

"They had a beautiful Mass. People came from all the communities, paying their tributes, giving their testimonies, singing songs, saying prayers. It really touched your heart. When the sun rose, we sang Josimo's favorite song — about angels coming to take your soul. He'd recently learned it, and he liked it so much, he told us he wanted to have it at his funeral.

"'For goodness sake, Josimo,' we used to say. 'Stop going on about death.' And he'd say, 'We're all going to die some day, that's for sure. If I die first, I want you to sing this song for me.' So we sang it at sunrise, and I could hardly get the words out.

"And then Domingos got into his car and drove to the edge of the river. All by himself. It was like he was saying his last farewell to Josimo."

"Here's how it was," Domingos told me. "Josimo and I often used to swim in the river in São Sebastião. We used to float down the river together. We both swam well. There's something highly symbolic about water as you know. The water of baptism, the water of life... And water has a particular significance in the Parrot's Beak. It's the land between the rivers, and the people who came here were fleeing from the droughts. There are a lot of legends in the dry lands about the Promised Land. It lies towards the sunset, and the great forest.

"Josimo was of the river people. He had a special affinity for the rivers. He used to call them the symbol of life. He even told me once that whoever is buried by the river will enter into the waters and give new life to the land. So that day, after the funeral, I went down to the river and I spoke to Josimo. I said, 'Well, Josimo, after all that, here you are by the river. And your spirit will move through the waters of this place. You will become part of the rivers that give life to this land, and you will be remembered for ever.'

"I felt I had to tell that to Josimo. And I had to go to the river. It was my farewell. Not that Josimo has gone. I believe in the existence of the soul, and for me Josimo isn't far away, he's here with us. In fact, I'm convinced he's a saint."

Chapter Seventeen

The Short Arm of the Law

On May 10th, 1986, as Josimo was shot on the steps of the
CPT office in downtown Imperatriz, the opening meeting of the
right-wing ranchers' union (UDR) was taking place at the Jussara
Club a few blocks away. Coincidence or not? Josimo wouldn't have
thought so. He was convinced the landowners were out to sabotage
land reform, and would do whatever they judged necessary to that
end.

With regard to the UDR, Josimo was right. Ostensibly, it was
a collection of large landowners who were determined to participate
in reshaping the government's original land reform plan launched
in May, 1985. In fact, the undeclared aim of the UDR was to frustrate
land reform by any and every means available to them — an aim in
which they succeeded brilliantly.

They financed themselves by auctioning off cattle, which they
had in very large numbers. As Josimo lay dying, the one hundred
and fifty founder members of the Imperatriz chapter of the UDR
raised the sum of one million cruzeiros ($40,000) by auction —
twenty times the price on the padre's head.

Josimo's friend and colleague, Padre Ricardo Resende, accused
the UDR of causing havoc in the Brazilian countryside, employing
private armies to carry out selective murders of labor leaders and
their supporters. To which Julimar de Queiroz, the brand-new UDR
chief in Imperatriz, retorted, "There are no such things as private
armies. They are quite unnecessary. We are not opposed to those
who need land."

The national boss of the UDR, Ronaldo Caiado, stated flatly
that the UDR had no connection whatsoever to the death of Padre
Josimo. The organization was composed of honorable and intelligent
men, he said, and they would never have recourse to gunmen. In
any case, Padre Josimo was no saint, but was known for inciting
rural violence, and was under police investigation for two offenses,
one of which was murder.

Caiado's number two, Salvador Farina, added that the UDR was not against land reform. It was created to collaborate with the government, principally in correcting the distortions of the first land reform plan, which the UDR considered as nothing more than a trial run. The second plan they saw as close to ideal. (After massive intervention by the UDR the second land reform plan emerged as a sickly shadow of the first.) "As practicing Christians," continued Farina, "we repudiate the wicked murder of Josimo. But we cannot forget the teaching that he who sows the wind reaps the whirlwind. This priest was victim of the hate and violence which he preached all his life."

Jorge Kalil Filho, UDR member from Imperatriz, maintained that the church and the UDR were twin souls. But apparently the bishops in the state of Maranhão did not agree. A week after Josimo's death, they excommunicated Jorge Kalil, together with the governor of Maranhão, Luiz Rocha; the Maranhão State Secretary of Public Security, Colonel Silva; the Maranhão UDR boss Hugo Saraiva, and all the UDR regional chiefs.

"In vain do they try to deceive the people by calling themselves Christians in favor of peace and love," thundered the bishops. "Let them give an account to the people of their land grabbing, of their impunity in the murder of the peasants, of the villages they have destroyed, and of the innumerable times they have violated the law and human rights."

The interdiction didn't bring about any drastic change in the attitude of the ranchers. At the Seventh Day Mass for Josimo held in São Sebastião, one of them remarked to a Goiás government secretary, "We have two options: either we kill them [the peasants] or they kill us."

The Brazilian Order of Lawyers pointed out that Josimo's murder was the tenth land-related death in Imperatriz in 60 days, and had no hesitation in identifying the culprits.

"Groups dissatisfied with the loss of their privileges have been giving repeated proofs that they plan to take the law into their own hands, wiping out those who defend the weak and the oppressed," they announced. "To do this, they create and maintain an infrastructure of organized crime, in terrorist actions which this year alone have victimized eighty-three people throughout Brazil."

The Goiás Workers' Party added its voice to the chorus of condemnation of the UDR. "It's clear that Josimo's death is related to the activities of the UDR, the terrorist entity which in broad daylight holds auctions with the object of buying arms and financing the criminal deeds of the large landowners."

The Vice President of the National Central of Trades Unions, Avelino Ganzer, went one further by stating, "Everything points to the resistance of the landowners as being something dreamed up and planned inside the government itself."

If Avelino Ganzer was correct in this assumption, it would explain the extraordinary laxity of the inquiry into the murder of Padre Josimo set up by the federal police.

Normally, murder cases fall within the jurisdiction of the state authorities, but there had already been various attempts to involve the federal police in this particular case. The bishops of the Center West had sought federal police intervention on April 30th after the first attack on Josimo. In February of that year, the Land Settlement Institute, INCRA, had also requested that the federal police be called in during land conflicts. Although no attempt had been made by government authorities to provide Josimo with any protection while he was still alive, they swung into action after he was safely out of the way. Two days after the murder, President Sarney announced that he was setting up a federal inquiry, headed by chief of police Romeu Tuma — a man who many in Brazil regarded with healthy skepticism. That he knew his job was beyond doubt. It was his antecedents that were open to question.

On May 13th, the president put full responsibility for coordinating government action to end rural violence into the hands of his Minister of Justice, Paulo Brossard. Since Minister Brossard was a large landowner (as was President Sarney himself), there were those who doubted that the peasants would get a fair deal.

Romeu Tuma, chief of Federal Police, held hearings in the nearby town of Marabá in the state of Pará, as well as in Imperatriz. He reported back to the president that he was operating in a context of robbery, land-grabbing, banditry and intense land conflict. Among those who testified were Colonel José Ribeira Silva, Maranhão State Secretary of Public Security, (a man who used to refer to his police chief as "my little sheriff" and was widely known for corruption), the prefect of Imperatriz, (ditto,) a delegation from GETAT and the two local military commanders. Romeu Tuma also heard from members of the Workers' and the Communist Parties, the base communities of the church, the bishops and the CPT.

The CPT stated that dozens of workers and agents were being assassinated every year, and until now, no one had been condemned for these crimes, although the identities of those responsible were common knowledge.

The military commander in Imperatriz painted a picture of impunity, corruption and massive siphoning off of funds with the collusion of municipal and state officials. The result was that the populace no longer trusted the authorities and was in a state of revolt. He added that the Imperatriz chief of civil police, Walber Dourado, was suspected of being hand in glove with local gunmen, as well as being involved with a gang of car thieves. The commandant described Josimo as an advocate for the landless, former local candidate for the Workers' Party, and under investigation for destruction of government property and for murder.

The commandant in Marabá confirmed his colleague's remarks about Padre Josimo, and also about the police chief, Walber Dourado. Walber Dourado in his turn said he was unable to improve the situation of law and order in the region because of shortage of men and materials. Of the 555 prosecutions brought in the previous three years, there had been just two murder convictions.

The prefect of Imperatriz had no explanation for the violence in his city but did state that even his police chief was scared.

Three days after the hearings, the General Secretary of the Ministry of Justice said that preliminary findings indicated probable participation of state civil and military police in land conflict violence, including the murder of Josimo. Federal Police Chief Tuma had some harsh words to say about the state authorities in Maranhão, Pará and Goiás, and blamed them for failing to put a stop to violent crime in the region. He even reported to the Minister of Justice that the civil and military police were conniving with the perpetrators of violence in the Parrot's Beak.

But local and state authorities demonstrated a sublime contempt for interference by the federal government, sending the Justice Minister a clear message to this effect when he called a meeting of governors of the seven states most affected by rural violence: Pará, Maranhão, Goiás, Mato Grosso, Mato Grosso do Sul, Bahia and Minas Gerais. In the previous sixteen months, these states had registered a combined total of 253 land conflict related deaths and Brossard felt it was time to do something about it. The Minister of Justice was attempting to clean up an area over half the size of the continental United States. Only two governors bothered to show up.

In a brave show of strength, the combined police forces had a two day crackdown in the region of the Parrot's Beak. They picked up a total of 500 arms, sixteen stolen cars and a large quantity of stolen and smuggled goods. CPT lawyer Agostinho Noleto was convinced that the disarming would serve no useful purpose. "Everyone here goes around armed," he said. "They have one revolver in the holster and a second in the glove compartment."

Imperatriz and the region of the Parrot's Beak were rapidly becoming the focus of national and even international attention. Newspaper articles referred to Imperatriz as the Chicago of Brazil, talked of the "law of the jungle," and painted an unflattering but not inaccurate picture of land disputes, gunmen, private armies, militant labor leaders, squatters, priests, agitators, communists and a situation bordering on civil war. Authorities and police were described as conniving or corrupt or both, and police were often featured on the crime pages — as criminals.

Imperatriz controlled an important road intersection, the newspapers pointed out, and no one in the town was immune from the gold fever of the nearby mines. The river towns of the Parrot's Beak had long been a refuge for outlaws and runaways, and the situation was worsening day by day as land-grabbers fell over one another to snap up land which could service the future industrial corridor of Carajás.

Local authorities were understandably sensitive about all this unwelcome publicity. The Goiás State Secretary of Public Security was unwilling to accept intervention from the federal police, stating repeatedly that he would only permit their presence if they came under his command. He categorically denied the existence of police violence in his state. Here, he was backed up by the state governor, who announced that his police had faithfully protected the life of Padre Josimo in the state of Goiás. He added that despite all figures to the contrary, deaths in his state connected with rural violence did not exceed one a year. Other deaths were wrongly attributed.

Imperatriz chief of military police, Raimundo Nonato Brandão, said that Josimo's death was a drop in the bucket in the context of land violence. He complained that it was getting increasingly difficult to deal with the situation of law and order because he had no help from the governor or the mayor. The truth was that he had been a little over-diligent during his six months in Imperatriz. He had arrested several *pistoleiros* and also a bunch of car thieves. For some reason, he appeared to have incurred the dislike of the Maranhão State Governor, the Secretary of Public Security, and the Chief of Civil Police. Shortly afterwards, alleging that it was impossible for him to work, he resigned.

Minister of Justice Paulo Brossard paid a visit to the area and accused the church of instigating land invasions. He also exonerated himself from the responsibility of making peace in the countryside by leaving it to the state police. His excuse was that he didn't have enough federal policemen available, and in any case he could only intervene if requested to. He was extremely alarmed to hear allegations that there were death squads in the countryside, and was most annoyed at one journalist's description of the situation in the Parrot's Beak as "a state of civil war." He did however concede, "Whether it's because of the geographical location or the distances, the fact is that in certain regions of Brazil, criminals enjoy virtual impunity."

Meanwhile, who killed Josimo? Why was no one arrested? The police concentrated their efforts on tracking down the license plates of the car — a move that could have proved futile had the gunmen bothered to fit their vehicle with false plates. It was this elementary mistake that led the police to Nenem, old enemy of Josimo. They concluded that it was a crime of revenge for the death of Donda — even though Donda had been killed almost three weeks after the first attack on Josimo. The police very nearly picked up Nenem, but he was lucky enough to escape -- some say thanks to the Goiás State Secretary of Security, Zé Freire. Ten years later, Nenem was still a free man. One of his brothers, João Teodoro da Silva, was arrested and jailed for several days, but finally released for "lack of proof."

Nearly four weeks passed before the police made their first significant breakthrough. They arrested Geraldo Rodrigues da Costa, the man who pulled the trigger.

Chapter Eighteen

Jailbirds and Jailbreaks

Geraldo was watching the ball game on TV when the police came for him. The owner of the house in Goiânia, Maria Aparecida Borges, had no idea that she was entertaining a murderer.

"He told me his name was Roberto," she told the police tearfully. "He was waiting to talk to my son Cidmir. It's not the first time he's been in the house. He told me they were working on a deal. Roberto was looking for a job. He said he was a tractor driver. I never thought he could be a murderer."

Geraldo had spent a few days hidden in Imperatriz with his accomplice Vilson, the one who drove the car. The pair of them then drove to Goiânia, stopping a couple of times en route to try to contact the Teodoro brothers. Geraldo wanted to collect the rest of his money and get out while the going was good. He even talked of going abroad.

The garage mechanic overheard Geraldo discussing the murder before it ever took place. When the Imperatriz police chief heard this particular detail, he remarked, "That wasn't just careless. It was unprofessional."

Though he already had a criminal record for armed robbery and was wanted in the south of the state, Geraldo certainly wasn't a skilled *pistoleiro*. He had failed to kill Josimo on at least two previous occasions, and even on the day of the murder, one of his two shots had gone wide of the mark.

Since making it to Goiânia, he had been hanging out at the Cafe Central looking for a job. It was there that he had met Cidmir and offered his services as a tractor driver. Cidmir must have had his doubts, for he had kept Geraldo waiting around for ten days. Geraldo had twice gone to Cidmir's house and no one had suspected anything out of the ordinary.

After arresting Geraldo, the police returned to search the house for arms, and to Maria Aparecida's surprise and alarm, they discovered a 7.65 mm pistol hidden in a glass bowl on the kitchen dresser. "He must have hidden it there earlier," she told them. "He did ask if he could make a telephone call, and it must have been then."

They took Geraldo to Imperatriz and put him in the town jail. But the chief of police didn't want him there. He complained to the judge that he only had one cell, and couldn't provide meals. So the judge sent the prisoner to the military barracks. It wasn't long before the commandant decided he didn't want him either. His excuse was that he wanted to paint out the cells. So the judge had to remove Geraldo and send him to the state penal colony at Pedrinhas.

The federal police chief of Goiás alleged that Geraldo was involved in drug smuggling with "Temtem" (Guiomar Teodoro da Silva), although it was never proved. But Geraldo did tell reporters that he had killed Josimo at the request of the brothers Temtem and Nenem, and later he mentioned other names: João Teodoro da Silva, Deca, Mundico, Geraldo (Nó), his son Adailson, and Arlindo Gomes de Souza.

Geraldo admitted that all the accusations against him were true. "It was Nenem who put me up to it," he said. "I was drinking with him one day and he asked me if I had the guts to kill Josimo. I said I wasn't sure, but he insisted. Later I met up with Vilson and Nó, and they persuaded me. We didn't settle on a price at that stage. Nenem always said it was no hassle because Josimo wasn't a proper padre, just a communist and a land invader."

The first time Geraldo saw Josimo, he didn't even recognize him. He'd been expecting a padre in a robe. Nenem wasn't at all pleased about that, and a few days later sent the *pistoleiros* a message to say that Josimo was in Augustinópolis having his car fixed. Vilson and Geraldo kept Josimo under close scrutiny, and followed him into the night.

It wasn't until the next day that Geraldo learned of Josimo's miraculous escape. He decided to head for Goiânia anyway, to give things a chance to cool down. In a couple of weeks he was back, and according to witnesses he and Vilson stayed very close to Josimo that last week. On the Wednesday, the news came through that Donda had died, and Nenem cursed and wept and swore to get Josimo. He sent for Geraldo and told him he was prepared to raise the price to 50,000 cruzeiros.

"I was drinking a lot at the time," Geraldo said. "And on the night of the 9th, I took a whole lot of pills as well. Saturday morning, Vilson came down to the bakery where I was having coffee and told me to get ready."

Geraldo told reporters he shot Josimo twice but he didn't know which bullet got him. He then crossed the crowded street with total lack of concern, ignoring the shoe-shine boy who told him his boots were dirty, climbed into the waiting car and sped away. "I was in no hurry," he said. "Did you ever see anyone round here go after a *pistoleiro*?"

He and Vilson spent the rest of the day celebrating, and Geraldo didn't come to his senses until the next morning. He then moved to another safe house for three days, and made his way unmolested back to Goiânia.

After his arrest, Geraldo was visited by Nó, who offered him a hundred thousand cruzeiros ($3500) to keep his and Temtem's names out of the case. Geraldo did as Nó asked but never received any payment, so he subsequently told on him.

In reply to one journalist, he declared, "I don't know if I killed a padre but I do know I killed a communist. Mind you, I was only the instrument. I pulled the trigger. There's a lot more people behind it. That's for the judge to sort out. It's not my problem. I know who's guilty, though. I know them all."

Geraldo may have known them all, but it did him little good. No serious attempts were made to indict any of them, and they remained free, while Geraldo stayed in jail — for a time.

His first attempt at escape was foiled by an honest prison guard. On November 11, 1986, Geraldo's lawyer, Jeova Morais, attempted to bribe the guard to let Geraldo go. Morais had misjudged his man and his request was refused, whereupon the lawyer asked if he could send in some liquor because he wanted to show that Geraldo was mentally unstable. Jeova said Geraldo was epileptic and shouldn't be held responsible, but medical tests found nothing wrong. At this point, Geraldo was moved to the military barracks and an inquiry was opened, whereupon the lawyer withdrew from the case.

Trial was set for 18 April, 1988, just over two years after the first attack on Josimo. In front of a packed house, the defense attorney referred to Josimo as a disobedient priest, a communist instigator of land invasions, a man who would be mourned only by his wives and children. At this point, Dona Cota from Esperantina leaped to her feet, waved her fist at the astonished attorney and shouted, "Lies!" The judge ordered her to sit down and be quiet.

After thirteen hours, sentence was passed. Geraldo was found guilty and sentenced to eighteen years and six months. His normally cocky manner had modified somewhat, and he professed to be repentant. The judge told him that if he behaved, his sentence might be shortened. Geraldo said he hoped the police would catch Nenem. "If they don't get Nenem," he said, "He'll continue his old tricks. It's easy to hire a *pistoleiro* round these parts."

Geraldo was sent to the state industrial penitentiary, CEPAIGO, located in Aparecida do Norte, Goiás. Although he was described as "highly dangerous," he was not placed in a high security jail. And he didn't stay there long. He was joined the following April by his accomplice, Vilson, who set to work to make himself agreeable to his jailers, rapidly upgrading his status to the point where he was granted leave of absence to visit his "sick" wife. He did not find it necessary to return from the visit.

On July 7th, 1990, Geraldo too made a break for it and was picked up three months later during the course of an armed robbery and abduction in Gurupi, a town located in the south of the new state of Tocantins (split off from Goiás.) By coincidence, Gurupi is the local seat of the CPT, and CPT staff were not convinced that the local jail would be able to hold Geraldo for long. They dispatched a volley of cables to local and state authorities, but despite all these, it was less than a week before Geraldo had escaped again.

The local judge stated he had wanted to keep Geraldo in Gurupi in order to give his testimony. Geraldo did not stay long enough for that. With the help of two bits of metal from his suitcase and a piece of wood, he was able to make a hole in the wall just underneath the roof — a place that had recently been reinforced following a previous attempted escape. The neighbors heard the noise and told the guards who were all out in the front, but they failed to intervene.

Accusations flew thick and fast. The chief of police said he had asked the judge to send Geraldo back to jail in Goiás, so it wasn't his fault. The judge said he was waiting to hear from the said jail, so it wasn't his fault, and anyway he was supposed to try the case in

Gurupi which was where the prisoner had been caught. He also added "Every criminal wants to escape." After that he took himself off on holiday, and his substitute had tried to have Geraldo sent to jail in nearby Porto Nacional, but they wouldn't have him. So it wasn't the deputy's fault either.

Barely four months later, on March 22nd, 1991, both Geraldo and Vilson were caught stealing cars in Minas Gerais. They were sent back to the CEPAIGO together, where they put their skills to good use by joining a gang of car thieves allegedly headed by camp commandant Colonel Nicola Limogi Filho. Of the two gunmen, it was certainly Vilson who made himself the more agreeable. He managed to obtain permission to visit his mother in the commandant's car, and was even permitted to travel without handcuffs. Once again, he saw no reason to return.

For some reason, the commandant did not find it necessary to inform anyone of the escape. It was only on the eve of Vilson's trial (June 15th, 1992) that an incredulous judge and an enraged CPT learned that the defendant had in fact escaped from jail nine months previously. Vilson has not been heard of since. Curiously enough, the day before his escape, a letter had arrived for the camp commandant referring to Vilson's part in the murder of Padre Josimo, and requesting that rigorous measures be taken to contain both Geraldo and Vilson. But Vilson has never stood trial, and it seems more than likely that he never will.

Meanwhile on December 17th, 1992, Geraldo was transferred to the military police in Goiás for safe-keeping. There is a very good chance that by the time you read this, he will have escaped again.

On March 13th, 1991, nearly five years after the crime, the following people were indicted in connection with the case of Padre Josimo: Geraldo Vieira (Nó), Adailson Vieira, Osmar Teodoro da Silva (Nenem), Guiomar Teodoro da Silva (Temtem), Nazaré Teodoro da Silva (Deca), and Oswaldo Teodoro da Silva (Mundico).

Nenem was spotted in São Sebastião three days after the crime. The police attempted to arrest him but he managed to escape – aided and abetted by the local State Deputy, Zé Freire. His lawyers then took out a writ of *habeas corpus* against possible preventive imprisonment, and Nenem went underground, as did his brother Temtem. Neither of them has been seen since then.

Geraldo Vieira, (Nó) was jailed but released for lack of evidence. He then went into hiding and was picked up again in August, 1994, together with his son, Adailson. In early 1997, they were still awaiting trial. Of the other members of the Teodoro da Silva family, Nenezão and Donda had already been killed before Josimo's murder and Joâo was later killed in a car crash. The driver (from a rival family of gunmen) ran for it, but was murdered four months later in the distant state of Roraima. As a result of this, Deca was the victim of an attempted assassination — which he survived. Deca and his brother Mundico are still living and practicing their profession in Buriti. They have both been indicted in the Josimo case, but are still at liberty.

An interesting commentary on Brazilian justice was the statement of the Goiás State Attorney General in the case brought by the CPT on behalf of Josimo's mother, Dona Olinda. They were attempting to sue the Federal Government and the State of Goiás for negligence in not providing protection for Padre Josimo despite repeated requests.

The federal government exonerated itself on the grounds that protection against violence is not in itself the responsibility of the union of states. They referred to Josimo as displaying a "provocative, recalcitrant and recidivistic attitude towards municipal and state authorities, which culminated in his own death." They pointed out that neither Josimo nor his superiors had taken any precautions after the first assassination attempt, and stated that Josimo had confronted the danger head on, "as though it was an inseparable part of his mission." Thus, in a final irony, the federal government considered that the victim himself was responsible for his own death.

The well known Brazilian attorney, Evaristo de Moraes Filho (later hired by then President Collor in his impeachment defense) said that Josimo's death had been inevitable from the moment he first took it upon himself to fight for the landless. Everyone knew that Josimo would die, everyone knew which groups would pay the killer. No one knew the hour, the day or the location. But the fact that the murder was committed in broad daylight in the center of the city proved that none of those involved in the murder expected to be arrested.

"The great and the powerful will never wipe out the poor," Josimo had written. "From their struggle will spring forth new life, a new world, a new earth and justice."

This new world with its new justice is not immediately apparent. Of the numerous people known to have been involved in the murder of Padre Josimo, only two have ever been convicted. How can this be, since everyone knows the identities of those involved?

The truth is that in Brazil, as in so many countries of the developing world, there is one justice for the rich and another for the poor. "You know who goes to prison in Brazil, don't you, dear?" a middle class lawyer once said to me at a party. "The three 'p's'. *'Pobre'* (poor) *'putas'* (prostitutes,) and *'pretos'* (blacks.) It's entirely predictable. The police are poorly educated, poorly equipped and poorly paid. It's only a question of time before they become corrupt. It may be little things, it may be big things. They use the rich man's car, they stay in his house, they haven't got their own transport, they often haven't even got the money to buy bullets.

"Then there's the friction between the police and the courts. The police often feel that they put a lot of effort into arresting people and the courts let them go. So the police aren't too concerned about how they get the evidence they need. It's a short step from a little roughing up to torture.

"There's another thing. The country is too big to run efficiently. Distances are too great, and infrastructure is practically non-existent. After the collapse of the military government, the federal government was determined to put the powers back into the hands of the states. That's fine if the states are in a position to run themselves efficiently. Some of them can — the southern states, São Paulo, Minas Gerais. But most of them just haven't got the structure, so the power goes right back where it came from — into the hands of the oligarchs, the landowning class that runs everything from politics to the police. And the oligarchs hang onto their power in the same way they always have: strong-arm methods. They get extremely upset when international attention suddenly focuses on them, like it did in the murder of the rubber tapper Chico Mendes. They can't see the justice of it. After all, they've been running things their way ever since the beginning, and they can't see why things should change. Justice? It's a luxury. I don't know that Brazil is ready for it."

Chapter Nineteen

One Law for the Rich

"Justice? It's a luxury."

I mulled over the lawyer's comment. Most citizens of developed countries feel that they can rely on their systems of justice. Despite exceptions, generally speaking they can expect the state to protect them against criminal violence. However, this is not so in most of the world. It is not so in Brazil. Imagine that you live in a country where, in addition to not being able to trust the police, you cannot trust the judiciary either. Suppose you live in a situation where, instead of the state protecting you from violence, you are forced to protect yourself. How do you defend yourself? Is the answer to buy a gun and hope that if there's any trouble, you will be first on the draw?

Brazil is far from being the world's worst offender in terms of human rights. There are as many decent, moral people in Brazil as anywhere else. At the time of Josimo's death, the Attorney General, Aristides Junqueira, was widely regarded as being above reproach, and there are many honorable and incorruptible lawyers and judges throughout the country. There are also some shining examples of honesty in the various police forces. Unhappily, there are many members of the police and the judiciary who are apathetic, inefficient, conniving, and corrupt. Consider the case of Josimo. Despite the fact that the bishops personally asked the President of the Republic for protection, delivered press releases showing the bullet holes in his Toyota, and succeeded in getting themselves maximum television coverage, nothing concrete was done. Ten days later, Josimo was gunned down. Not that police protection would have necessarily have provided any guarantee. Chico Mendes had police guards. They did not save his life.

There are three different police forces in Brazil: civil, military and federal. The federal police are responsible for interstate smuggling, drug trafficking and interstate slavery — a category of crime which has increased dramatically in the last two or three years. They are also empowered to step in when a crime has national implications, or when state police are being manifestly incompetent. This is a right which they are notably reluctant to exercise unless sufficiently pressured.

The military police are responsible for day to day policing. They are frequently criticized for indulging in excessive force, unlawful arrests and torture. Naturally this affects the poor rather than the rich, partly because the poor are less able to defend themselves, and partly because the press tends to describe them as armed, treacherous, lazy and stupid. In the case of the Parrot's Beak they are also considered to be communists, which makes them doubly dangerous.

The police may not have a high standard of education but they are smart enough to know that it is not worth their while to go after the rich. The rich can hire lawyers who can tell them how to take advantage of the Lei Fleury, which says that you may not be held in custody unless caught *'in flagrante.'* If you have no criminal antecedents, you can also await trial at liberty. (If you are seriously worried about the outcome, this will give you ample opportunity to skip town, or disappear across the nearest state border. With luck, no one will trouble you further.) If by any misfortune you are convicted, you will qualify for a better standard of accommodation than your fellows, particularly if you can claim to have had a university education. In any case, the military police do not deal in criminal investigations. That is the job of the civil police. All the police forces complain of low salaries, and it is not unusual to find a chief of police running a large district with practically no equipment. Walber Dourado, chief of police in Imperatriz, told critics that he was running a district of 2,250 square miles. He had 100 military policemen, 41 civil policemen and three cars, of which two were broken. There was an average of one reported murder a day.

Regulations require the civil police chief to be a law graduate, but in practice this requirement is waived in many rural areas where the chiefs of police are sloppy, untrained and often corrupt. Generally speaking, they are unable or unwilling to prosecute members of the local elite. They may be forced to make a token arrest, but suspects are usually quickly released "for lack of evidence." In one notorious case, Pedro Vieira, police chief of Rio

Maria, Pará, sat on his hands after a series of political assassinations of union leaders -- old adversaries of his whom he had tried several times to put behind bars but had been forced to release because he couldn't pin anything on them. After four such murders in the space of three weeks in 1990, he was relieved of his post by the state governor. His substitute, Eleovaldo de Jesus Miranda de Souza, was considered to have compromised his ability to dispense impartial justice after accepting gifts of food and housing from the mayor. Shortly afterwards he was retired "for health reasons."

Even urban police chiefs are frequently hand in glove with the local elites. The Maranhão State Secretary of Public Security, José Silva Ribeiro, used to call his police force "my little policemen," and laughingly referred to the Imperatriz police chief as "my little sheriff." The said little sheriff (Walber Dourado) was widely considered to be corrupt and alleged to be up to his ears in car theft.

The inventory of police inefficiency makes depressing reading. Crimes are incorrectly registered, registered too late, or not registered at all. Investigations are mounted with paralyzing slowness, witnesses are not interviewed, suspects are not arrested, forensic and ballistic exams are not done, postmortems are not conducted. Investigations are incompetently handled, and frequently not completed on time -- which means they are annulled. Dossiers, files and documents of every sort disappear, inquests are derailed for frivolous reasons, and in the few cases of arrest it is always the gunmen, never those who hire them, who land up behind bars. Even so, cases of escape are common.

In almost any town in Brazil, it won't take you long to find out who the local *pistoleiros* are. Most people own a weapon of some sort, and if you want to, you can probably discover who is next on the hit list. The law says you must register a hand gun, but the police themselves admit that 99% of weapons carried in Brazil are unregistered. The law also states that you may defend your property with weapons if necessary. You can therefore defend your land, and by extension, the land you claim. From here, it is a short step to considering the right of property as more important than human rights.

To give you some idea of the stranglehold that the oligarchs held (and sometimes still hold) over the ordinary people, you need look no further than the political situation five years ago in the city of Marabá in the state of Pará. Marabá lies less than a hundred and fifty miles from Imperatriz where Josimo was murdered, and it is not the place for a quiet retirement. It is a place better avoided altogether, since until recently it was run as a feudal domain by a particularly notorious family called Mutran.

Doyen of the family was Oswaldo Mutran, state deputy for the Social Democrat Party. He was known as Vavá. His brother, Guido, was a town councilman, and his son, Nagib, was the mayor of Marabá.

The man who blew the whistle on the Mutrans was Vavá's former driver, Joatan Ribeiro Lima. Joatan was a brave man for testifying, and he was fully aware of the risks involved. In November, 1991, he escaped from a private jail where the Mutrans had been holding him, and he had plenty to say about his former employers. He denounced them to the federal police in Marabá, to the Attorney General of the Republic, and to the Parliamentary Commission on Rural Violence.

Joatan accused the Mutrans of being behind the killings of at least eleven rural workers. He said that he had witnessed the killing of a worker called Neguinho on one of Vavá's properties, Fazenda Virasebo. He alleged that there were clandestine cemeteries on Fazenda Virasebo and on Fazenda Jequibaia (which belonged to Vavá's brother, Guido). The driver testified for nine hours, backed his claims with a 300 page document, and then asked for federal protection because he feared for his life.

More evidence about the Mutrans was presented at the same parliamentary commission. The Workers' Party (PT) had a complete dossier on the family. It mentioned, among other things, that Vavá had several times invaded the town hall to attack or threaten opposition city council members, and that his brother, councilman Guido, had sworn to kill five of his fellow councilmen. Vavá had also threatened state deputy Edmilson Rodrigues. Indeed, the Marabá police had received six complaints about Vavá, alleging physical and verbal aggression and death threats. Among those threatened were a priest and a television reporter.

Joatan, the driver, added that criminal prosecutions were thwarted because Ezilda Pastana, a judge in Marabá, was the common-law wife of Vavá's son, Oswaldo Jr., who was also brother to the mayor, Nagib.

Of the twelve land conflicts registered by the CPT in Marabá from 1976 to 1984, five involved the Mutran family, accused of everything from threats and beatings to ordering the killing of squatters.

In 1988, the *Jornal do Brasil* reported that Sebastião de Terezona — now in jail and accused of at least 50 murders — confessed to having worked for Vavá and his brother Aziz. He also said that Vavá and José Edmundo Ortiz Vergolino were responsible for the massacre of nine people in a nut grove in Sao Joâo de Araguaia in 1985.

And then another scandal broke in Marabá involving the Mutrans. The mayor, Nagib, was using child labor to clean the city streets and the kids were subjected to sexual abuse as a condition for receiving their paltry salaries. This was taking place in the presence of Vavá. The story ran in Brazil's most important newspaper, the *Folha de São Paulo*, and the mayor reacted by firing the children and hiring others, this time over sixteen years of age.

Vavá was summoned to give a statement to the parliamentary commission in November, 1991. These commissions have no power to prosecute, but they can draft federal legislation, make recommendations and bring public attention to national problems. Mutran denied all the allegations against him, calling them a bunch of lies from start to finish. He said it was a plot by his enemies. He even managed to produce a police certificate to prove that there wasn't a single charge outstanding against him. He was extremely chagrined when Pará state deputy Giovanni Queiroz came up with a document from the Marabá police confirming that there were in fact several criminal charges against Vavá. That day Queiroz's wife received two anonymous calls referring to her husband as "the deceased."

The First Assistant Attorney General, Alvaro Ribeiro Costa, asked the Minister of Justice to ensure that the federal police open an inquiry, but a few days later the Marabá Federal Police chief Jose Herman Almeida told the *Folha de São Paulo* that he had done nothing.

Journalists from the *Folha* then decided to look into the allegations about clandestine cemeteries. In the cemetery of Novo Marabá, they found dozens of unmarked graves. Clodomiro Siqueira, the grave digger, said that he had been working there for six years, and that during that time he had buried more than one thousand unidentified bodies. He said that they were all peasants, and that forty percent of them had been murdered. "It's the Mutrans who order these people to be buried," he added.

At this point the federal police chief, Jose Herman Almeida, passed the buck to the chief of civil police, Antonio Puxias, who retorted that it was a job for the federal police. Whereupon Vavá issued them with a warm invitation to inspect any of his properties.

By the following April, Vavá was back at his old tricks. A truckload of his cattle had been detained for non-payment of taxes, and Vavá and three of his buddies invaded the house of the official responsible, and slaughtered him. This was too much even for the long suffering people of Marabá. More than five thousand of them staged a protest, demanding that Vavá be sacked as state deputy, arrested and punished.

Nonetheless, Vavá went on to win election as state deputy after his term as mayor. Not until an impeachment case was brought against him by the local revenue department, citing repeated violence towards them by Vavá and his henchmen, did Vavá vanish from the public eye.

In the end, the people of a nation must take responsibility for their own society. International pressure may shame a dilatory judicial system to convict the killers of Chico Mendes or Padre Josimo, but it will be up to the Brazilians themselves to see that Brazilian justice guarantees, not one law for the rich and one law for the poor, but one law for all.

Chapter Twenty

Death, Be Not Proud

"Well, Amparo," I said, as she and I huddled together in front of a noisy but ineffectual air conditioner on a breathless afternoon in Imperatriz. "You worked with Josimo. You were there when he died. Looking back on now, was it all worth it? Did you achieve what you wanted? And what about Josimo? Did he sacrifice his life for nothing?"

"It's a thing I often think about," Amparo looked thoughtfully into her coffee cup. "Let's start with Josimo. A lot of the simple people think he was a saint. They pray to him, and I guess it does no harm. They even say he does miracles. But I don't think he was a saint. And he certainly wasn't a martyr. I was furious at his funeral when some of the padres started talking about the blood of martyrs nourishing new life. They told us that new workers would come to the harvest. I thought, you fools, you're quite wrong. No one else will come.

"We are very few, you know. If they kill one of our best, it's as if they killed a thousand. We'll never find another Josimo. They murdered him and they murdered the hopes of thousands. We don't have a lot of people. Others don't come to take our place. It's a nice theory, but it isn't true."

"Did you give up, Amparo?" I said softly.

"No," said Amparo. "I didn't give up. You probably think I sound very pessimistic. I didn't give up. But Josimo's death was the end of something, and there's no way he's going to come back. It was an ending for me, and for a lot of other people too. We didn't just lose Josimo. We lost our courage. We lost our youth, in a sense. All those years gone. We worked ourselves into the ground. We lived very intensely. There was no time for a normal life. We were always under the shadow of death — even though somehow we never expected it would happen.

"Then, when it did, where was the resurrection? We won some of the land, but nothing really changed. People in the Parrot's Beak today don't live any better than they did before. They don't eat better or dress better, they still don't wear shoes. They work so hard, and they get nowhere. They live such wretched lives. I think it's a question of culture. The squatters live for the moment. They're fatalists. If things go wrong, they say it's the will of God. Like all peasants, they're very conservative. They do what their fathers did.

"Take the matter of crops. They've got it in their heads that the only thing they can plant here is rice. That's not true, this land will grow lots of things. But they won't plant other things, they don't produce any more, and they don't live any better.

"It makes me angry, sometimes. They've got the land. Good land, too. If a man has fifty acres here, he should be rich. He should be able to live well for the rest of his life. He can keep his cow, his pig for fattening, and his chickens. He can grow everything he needs -- coffee, sugar, corn, manioc, rice, beans, fruit, vegetables. Instead of which, he lives in extreme poverty. You can go to his house and you won't find anything to eat.

"It's true he gets no incentive to change. No help, no infrastructure. No technical assistance. We should have technicians here showing him how to plant peanuts, potatoes, fruits like *cupuaçu* or *acaí*. We should encourage him to go all out for capitalism. After all, the people here are all very individualistic. They live together, but they've got no spirit of community. I think we should be trying to foster an entrepreneurial spirit. Let's be out and out capitalists. There's nothing immoral in that. Let's make a go of it, and then perhaps they'll pull themselves out of this misery."

"Do you think the church chose the wrong path in preaching socialism?" I asked.

"Yes, I think it did," she said, without hesitation. "You can't create a socialist utopia overnight. You can't take a peasant from the backwoods and turn him into a community-minded Christian, just like that. We've got the land but we have to change our relationship to it, and to each other. I think we're going backwards. We're never going to have a revolution in this place. We can't transform capitalism into socialism without a revolution, and there's not going to be a revolution. There's no reason why we can't produce, and sell and live well, without exploiting others. People here don't think ahead. If we have enough for today, let's not worry about tomorrow, that's how they think. It's beautiful, but it's not real. The world has changed. It isn't tiny any more. It's very complex.

"Sometimes I think Josimo died for nothing. Such an extraordinary man, and his life just snuffed out like that. What a waste of a life! Then I get to thinking: did we all waste our lives? We gave up a lot, you know. We gave up our time, our energy, our youth. We lived hard, we felt we had a mission. It didn't leave time for anything else. We didn't get round to doing normal things like getting married and having babies. And I don't think we really changed anything."

I put the question to the bishop. "I understand what Amparo means," he said, a trifle sadly. "But you have to try and see the whole picture. There have been a lot of changes, partly because this area was made into a new state. In Josimo's day, we were at the back of beyond, the far north of the state of Goiás. But now we're in the state of Tocantins, a brand new state. So there's a lot more money about. More staff for the police force and the judiciary, more money for the townships, electricity, telephones, even for things like the roads, believe it or not. You may not think our roads are up to much but they're a lot better than they used to be.

"But I'd say that the greatest change has been in the people. They've begun to realize what they can do: the base communities, the unions, the women's associations, all the ways in which people work together. They've got the land, and now some of them are giving serious thought to the question of how they're going to stay on it. They have a much greater awareness of their rights. They're prepared to stand up for themselves, and that's only since Josimo and his team started telling them they were human beings and not slaves.

"Of course, politically, things are much easier these days. We're not living under a dictatorship any more. And we've got a new constitution. And a model constitution it is, too, even if it is a bit complex. People say that Brazil has the best laws in the world! It's just a question of enforcing them.

"On the question of human rights — there's been a lot of international pressure, and that forces governments into action. Amnesty International, Americas Watch, foreign governments, the United Nations — the more the better. It reinforces our own human rights groups. Political awareness is growing all the time. You have to remember that when Josimo died, we were only just emerging from twenty years of military dictatorship. No one had any political education at all.

"So if you asked me whether it was all worth it, I'd say yes. We achieved a lot. Not just in terms of land, but in the changes that happened to the people. They've been downtrodden for centuries. All that time, the church had been paternalistic, giving handouts here and there, but still keeping people dependent. Then all of a sudden everything changed, and instead of giving handouts, we were trying to make people take charge of their own destiny, and be responsible for their own actions. It's a way of growing that's highly complex and difficult to do, and the people found it an enormous challenge. But some of them managed it. They discovered that they could take charge of their lives, and that's a thing that won't be stopped. So now, slowly, hesitantly, they are beginning to come into their own. They are calling a halt to exploitation. That's an extraordinary achievement."

I went to Sampaio to see what the people themselves had to say. Natividade had no hesitation. "Of course it was worth it!" she declared. "We've done the most difficult thing. We got the land. It wouldn't have happened if Josimo hadn't died. I'm convinced of that. We'd been pestering GETAT for years, we'd been to Brasília with Josimo, and we got promises here, promises there, yet hardly any action. But somehow after Josimo died, it was like there was no stopping us. People from all over the country started supporting us. So we decided to ask the president to give us our land. Josimo had lost his life for it, and we weren't going to let him die for nothing. 'We're going down to see the president,' we said, 'and we're not leaving until he gives us our land.'

"We went down to Brasília. There were four hundred of us. I remember we went to the Council of Bishops very early in the morning and after that we tried to get into that big main street where the government lives. All of a sudden, they sent in the riot police armed with shields and helmets, with the most horrible looking dogs. You'd have thought they were out to put down a revolution or something. All we wanted was our land. They said we couldn't go any further, but we hadn't come all that way just to be stopped.

We'd expected something of the sort, so we had our plans all ready. We'd decided the best thing to do was for us all to arrive together. Some of the women got out of the bus and told the police they had to find a bathroom. Before the police knew what was happening, we were all out, and they were completely surrounded. We were all wearing our white head scarves with Josimo's name embroidered on them. Raimunda started singing, we all joined in, and then we started marching down towards the congress building. I heard one of the policemen say, 'A woman can trick the Devil himself!' So we went off to ask the president to give us our land.

"There were people from the newspapers and the television all over the place, and I think the police were scared to stop us. We stayed a long time in Brasília, we must have visited almost all the ministries, even though they said they wouldn't talk to us. So we just sat down and said we weren't moving until they did, and in the end they were so fed up, they gave in. We got a lot of the land expropriated. Not all of it, but we'll keep on at them, and we'll get there in the end."

Dona Raimunda was equally positive. "What did we achieve? The land!" she told me emphatically. "That's what we were after, wasn't it? And we got it. Now this place here is a bit different from the others. We've got a communal title, and I'll tell you why. It's quite simple. People in this community were thrown off their lands, and the same thing happened to our neighbors in São Francisco. We fought shoulder to shoulder for the land, and they got theirs. But we didn't. After they'd got their land, do you suppose they helped us out at all? Not at all. They wouldn't let us near the babassu trees, wouldn't allow us to collect firewood, wouldn't let us make charcoal, wouldn't let us do anything. So we thought, if this is what is going to happen, we'd better do things differently when we get our land. We saw that land divided means people divided. So when we finally got our own land, we sat down and decided to keep it for the community. Everyone gets to put his fields where he wants, and we have communal fields too. And we don't let anyone sell up. If they want to leave they can, but they can't sell the land. We'll pay them for the improvements they make, but the land stays with the community.

"We have our own rules too. If we have an internal problem, we don't call in the police. We resolve it ourselves. We take our decisions communally, and if someone does something wrong, we have a meeting to discuss it. Working and living in community isn't easy; it takes a lot of patience. If people talk bad, you have to resist the temptation to talk back. We only succeed because we are a small community -- thirty families at the moment. We have eight hundred and fifty acres and we're living well. We're taking our own decisions, we're making our own mistakes, and we're in charge of our own lives."

Pedro Tierra was a special friend of Josimo's and as deeply committed as Josimo to the people's struggle. "So, Pedro," I asked him. "Did things really change?"

Pedro looked at me hard. "Did things change? Some things did, some didn't. The violence has diminished a lot, there's no doubt about that. But it's something that's endemic, somehow, to the place. It's woven into the fabric of their lives. It expresses itself in so many ways: child prostitution, wife beating, drinking, fighting, killing each other. These days the battle front is moving west across the Araguaia river into southern Pará. That's where you'll see the total disregard for human life that you used to see here in the Parrot's Beak. It's partly because of the gold mines. They attract all sorts of undesirable characters from all walks of life. There are old fashioned despots there like the Mutrans in Marabá. It's becoming more and more common to hear of cases of slavery on the big ranches. So that's where the Josimos of today are to be found.

"Not that I want to give you the impression that you can easily find people like Josimo. You can't. Josimo was very rare and very precious, and we mustn't ever underestimate the loss we suffered at his death. If he had been alive today, the Parrot's Beak would have been a very different place. His death was a great defeat."

And then I returned to Josimo's country and I went, as he must have done so many times, to the small wooden union building in Buriti.

We sat round in the uncertain light of an oil lamp, and I saw before me the men and women who were the protagonists of this ongoing struggle.

"So," said I. "Was it worth it all?"

There was a long silence.

"Well," said one old man, "We won a few battles. And it's important to remember where we came from. We had nothing. No land, no hope, no nothing. Now, at least, we've won the land."

"Lots of us have left it, though," pointed out the woman in the corner.

"That's true," said the old man, "But a lot of us are still there. We're not making a fortune, but we're making a decent living."

"We can sleep soundly in our beds," said another woman.

"And we're beginning to try out new things," added a young man.

"Yes," said the old man. "We need to do that, so we'll have something to sell. We've got a good bull now, and a community tractor. We're trying out different varieties of seeds, and even talking about doing things we've never done before."

"Like the bees," said another man. "I've got three hives and I'm producing a lot of honey. Carlinhos is selling it for me, and I'm going to put in another three hives as soon as I can."

"There's another thing," said a man with a straw hat, who had been listening attentively. "We've got our union. It was Josimo who kept telling us that we must get together to fight for our rights. We had a terrible time getting the unions set up. Over in Augustinópolis the *pistoleiros* shot up the meeting we were having in the church to talk about setting up the union, and the police beat the daylights out of the men in Sampaio at their meeting."

"There's been a lot of internal fighting," added the young man. "The mayor we've got here now, Joâo Olímpio, he's doing his level best to get control of the union. But he's not going to succeed, and now we're working in São Sebastião to set up a union there."

"We've got the Women's Association of Babassu Gatherers," put in the woman in the corner.

"And don't forget the Workers' Party," said the other woman.

"It all started out of the base communities," mused the old man.

"That's true enough," said Straw Hat. "When Padre Josimo came, it was really the first time we'd taken part in the church."

"He included everybody," said the woman in the corner. "Before he came, we women stayed in the background, hardly opening our mouths. Suddenly Josimo had us all taking part, just the same as the men."

"It was like he lit a light for us," said the other woman. "He showed us so many things. He showed us how to live together, how to work together, how to pray together..."

"What happened after Josimo died?" I inquired. "Did things go on the same, or did they fall back?"

"They fell back a lot," said the old man. "But they didn't stop. I don't think they could stop now, after all we've done together. Some people got discouraged and left. But Josimo always used to say that good things take time to grow. He always used to say, for instance, that one day the people of São Sebastião would understand what we were trying to do, and I believe they do, some of them. They wouldn't be setting up a union, if they didn't understand."

"So we've got the base communities," said the young man.

"And the union," said the woman in the corner.

"And the Workers' Party," added Straw Hat.

"And the land," said the old man.

"Is this all thanks to Josimo?" I looked round the circle of intent faces.

"Well," said Straw Hat, "It wasn't only Josimo. It was the Sisters too."

"And Nicola," added the old man.

"And Lurdinha,"

"And the CPT,"

"And what about us?" said Straw Hat. "It wouldn't have happened without us. I reckon we are the heroes of the story too, both those of us who are still around, and those of us who have gone."

"Like Josimo," said the woman in the corner.

"Like Josimo," echoed the old man sadly.

THE END

◆ Bibliography ◆

Aldighieri, Mario: *Josimo: Uma Vida no Conflito Social do Bico de Papagaio.*

Americas Watch: *Rural Violence in Brazil.* New York, 1991.

Americas Watch: *The Struggle for Land in Brazil: Rural Violence Continues.* New York, 1992.

Amnesty International: *Brazil, Authorised Violence in Rural Areas.* London, 1988.

Boff, Leonardo: *Igreja, Carisma e Poder.* Editora Vozes, Petropolis, 1981.

Boff, Leonardo: *Teologia do Cativeiro e da Libertação.* Editora Vozes, Petropolis, 1985.

Boff, Leonardo: *Ecclesiogenesis.* Editora Vozes, Petrópolis, 1986.

Commissão Pastoral da Terra: *Conflitos no Campo 1984-1993.* CPT, Goiãnia, 1986.

Commissão Pastoral da Terra: *Padre Josimo: A Vêlha Violencia da Nova República.* CPT, Goiania, 1986.

Conferência Nacional dos Bispos do Brasil: *Igreja e Problemas da Terra.* Edições Paulinas, São Paulo, 1990.

Diocese de Tócantinopolis: *Voz do Norte.* Imperatriz, 1986.

Federação de Assistência Social e Económica: *Dossié duma Morte Anunciada.* FASE, Rio, 1987.

FASE: *Que Brasil é este?* Rio, 1991.

Federal Government of Brazil: *Parliamentary Inquiry into Rural Violence.* Brasília, 1992.

Feres, Joao Bosco: *Propriedade da Terra - Opressão e Miséria .* CEDLA, São Paulo

Figueira, Ricardo Resende: *A Justiça do Lobo.* Editora Vozes. Petrópolis, 1986.

Figueira, Ricardo Resende: *Rio Maria - Canto da Terra .* Editora Vozes. Petrópolis, 1982.

Food and Agriculture Organisation of the United Nations: *Principal Socio-Economic Indicators of Colonisation in Land Reform*. FAO, Brasília, 1992.

MacDonald, Neil: *Brazil, A Mask called Progress*. Oxfam, Oxford, 1991.

Martins, Jose de Souza: *Não Há Terra Para Plantar Neste Verão*. Editora Vozes, Petrópolis, 1986.

Minc, Carlos: *A Reconquista da Terra - Lutas no Campo e Reforma Agrária*. Editora Jorge Zakar, São Paulo.

Movimento dos Trabalhadores Sem Terra: *Assassinatos no Campo - Crime e Impunidade 1964-86*. São Paulo, Editora Global, 1987.

Ordem dos Advogados do Brasil: *Violência no Campo*. OAB, Rio, 1986.

Procopio Filho, Argemir: *Posseiros e Colonos: A Luta pela Vida no Médio Araguaia*. Fundação Universidade de Brasília, Brasília 1985.

Da Silva, Jose Graziano: *Reforma Agrária da Nova Republica - Contradições e Alternativas*. EDUC, São Paulo.

◆ INDEX ◆